SISTER BERNADETTE'S BARKING DOG

THE QUIRKY HISTORY AND LOST ART OF DIAGRAMMING SENTENCES | BY KITTY BURNS FLOREY

MELVILLE HOUSE PUBLISHING
HOBOKEN, NEW JERSEY

©2006 KITTY BURNS FLOREY

BOOK DESIGN:
DAVID KONOPKA

ILLUSTRATION:
JOEL HOLLAND,
WWW.JMHILLUSTRATION.COM

MELVILLE HOUSE PUBLISHING
300 OBSERVER HIGHWAY
THIRD FLOOR
HOBOKEN, NEW JERSEY 07030

WWW.MHPBOOKS.COM

FIRST MELVILLE HOUSE PRINTING
OCTOBER 2006
ISBN 10: 1-933633-10-7
ISBN 13: 978-1-933633-10-7

Portions of this book first appeared in an altered form in
The Vocabula Review, Harper's Magazine, and *Best American
Essays 2005,* edited by Susan Orlean and published by
Houghton Mifflin.

Photo of Brainerd Kellogg used by permission of the
Polytechnic University Archives.

The photo "Alonzo Reed and his wife in front of Seatuck Lodge"
is from *A History of Remsenburg* (2003) published by and
used with the permission of The Remsenburg Association, Inc.

The photo "Gertrude Stein and one of the Baskets" is courtesy of
The Yale Collection of American Literature, Beinecke Rare Book
and Manuscript Library, Yale University.

The photographs on page 147 are courtesy of Maya Fineberg.

The poem "A Dog" from *Tender Buttons* ©1914
by Gertrude Stein is used by permission of Stanford G. Gann, Jr.,
Literary Executor of the Estate of Gertrude Stein.

LIBRARY OF CONGRESS CATALOGING-IN-PUBLICATION DATA

Florey, Kitty Burns.
Sister Bernadette's barking dog : the quirky history and lost
art of diagramming sentences / Kitty Burns Florey.
    p. cm.
  ISBN-13: 978-1-933633-10-7 (alk. paper)
  ISBN-10: 1-933633-10-7 (alk. paper)
  1. English language—Sentences. 2. English language—
Grammar. 3. English language—Syntax. I. Title.
PE1375F56 2006
428.2—dc22
                                        2006024703

SISTER BERNADETTE'S
BARKING DOG

chapter 1

ENTER THE DOG

Diagramming sentences is one of those lost skills, like darning socks or playing the sackbut, that no one seems to miss. When it was introduced in an 1877 text called *Higher Lessons in English* by Alonzo Reed and Brainerd Kellogg, it swept through American public schools like the measles, embraced by teachers as the way to reform students who were engaged in (to take Henry Higgins slightly out of context) "the cold-blooded murder of the English tongue." By promoting the beautifully logical rules of syntax, diagramming would root out evils like "him and me went" and "I ain't got none," until everyone wrote like Ralph Waldo Emerson, or at least James Fenimore Cooper.[1]

Even in my own youth, many years after 1877, diagramming was serious business. I learned it in the sixth grade from Sister Bernadette.

1   I'm thinking here of Mark Twain's famous and still highly entertaining essay, "Fenimore Cooper's Literary Offenses," in which Twain concludes that "in the restricted space of two-thirds of a page, Cooper has scored 114 literary offenses out of a possible 115. It breaks the record." But Wilkie Collins called Cooper "the greatest artist in the domain of romantic fiction in America."

Sister Bernadette: I can still see her, a tiny nun with a sharp pink nose, confidently drawing a dead-straight horizontal line like a highway across the blackboard, flourishing her chalk in the air at the end of it, her veil flipping out behind her as she turned back to the class. *We begin*, she said, *with a straight line*. And then, in her firm and saintly script, she put words on the line, a noun and a verb—probably something like *dog barked*. Between the words she drew a short vertical slash, bisecting the line. Then she drew a road—a short country lane—that forked off at an angle under the word *dog*, and on it she wrote *The*.

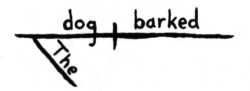

That was it: subject, predicate, and the little modifying article that civilized the sentence—all of it made into a picture that was every bit as clear and informative as an actual portrait of a beagle in mid-woof. The thrilling part was that this was a picture not of the animal but of the words that stood for the animal and its noises. It was a representation of something that was both concrete (we could hear the words if we said them aloud, and they conveyed an actual event) and abstract (the words were invisible, and their sounds vanished from the air as soon as they were uttered). The diagram was the bridge between a dog and the description of a dog. It was a bit like art, a bit like mathematics. It was much more than words uttered, or words written on a piece of paper: it was a picture of language.

I was hooked. So, it seems, were many of my contemporaries. Among the myths that have attached themselves to memories of being educated in the '50s is the notion that activities like diagramming sentences (along with memorizing poems and adding long columns of figures without a calculator) were draggy and monotonous. I thought diagramming was fun, and most of my friends who were subjected to it look back with varying degrees of delight. Some of us were better at it than others, but it was considered a kind of treat, a game that broke up the school day. You took a sentence, threw it against the wall, picked up the pieces, and put them together again, slotting each word into its pigeonhole. When you got it right, you made order and sense out of what we used all the time and took for granted: sentences. Those ephemeral words didn't just fade away in the air but became chiseled in stone—yes, this is a sentence, this is what it's made of, this is what it looks like, a chunk of English you can see and grab onto.

I remember loving the look of the sentences, short or long, once they were tidied into diagrams—the curious geometric shapes they made, their maplike tentacles, the way the words settled primly along their horizontals like houses on a road, the way some roads were *culs de sac* and some were long meandering interstates with many exit ramps and scenic lookouts. And the perfection of it all, the ease with which—once they were laid open, all their secrets exposed—those sentences could be comprehended.

On a more trivial, pre-teen level, part of the fun was being summoned to the blackboard to show off your skills. There you'd be with your chalk while, with a glint in her eye, Sister Bernadette read off an especially tricky sentence. Compact, fastidious handwriting was an asset. A good spatial sense helped you arrange things so that the diagram didn't end up jammed against the edge of the blackboard like commuters in a subway car. The trick was to think fast, write fast, and try not to get rattled if you failed nobly in the attempt.

As we became more proficient, the tasks got harder. There was great appeal in the Shaker-like simplicity of sentences like *The dog chased the rabbit* (subject, predicate, direct object) with their plain, no-nonsense diagrams:

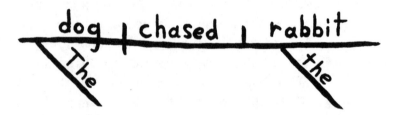

But there were also lovable subtleties, like the way the line that set off a predicate adjective slanted back toward the subject it referred to, like a signpost or a pointing finger:

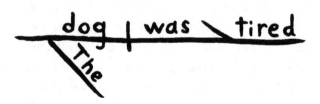

Or the thorny rosebush created by diagramming a prepositional phrase modifying another prepositional phrase:

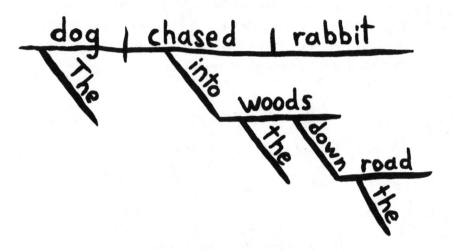

Or the elegant absence of the preposition with an indirect object, indicated by a short road with no house on it:

2   In this case, Sister B. departed slightly from Reed & Kellogg and from most traditional diagrammers, who would express the implied "you" with the less interesting and more generic "x." X would probably stand in for "to" in the preceding example as well.

The missing preposition—in this case *to*—could also be indicated by placing it on that road with parentheses around it, but this always seemed to me a clumsy solution, right up there with explaining a pun. In a related situation, however, the void where the subject of an imperative sentence would go is better filled—in my opinion then and now—with the graphic and slightly menacing parenthesized pronoun,[2] as in:

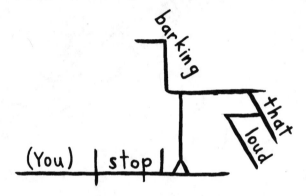

Stop that loud barking!

Questions were a special case: for diagramming, they had to be turned inside out, the way a sock has to be eased onto a foot: *What is the dog doing?* transformed into the more dramatic:

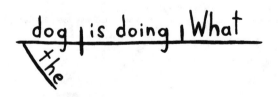

The dog is doing what?

Mostly we diagrammed sentences out of a grammar book, but sometimes we were assigned the task of making up our own, taking pleasure in coming up with wild Proustian wanderings that—kicking and screaming—had to be corralled, harnessed, and made to trot in neat rows into the barn.

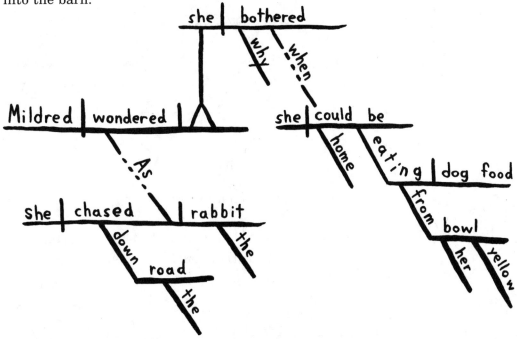

We hung those sentences out like a wash, wrote them like lines of music, arranged them on a connecting web of veins and arteries until we understood every piece of them. We could see for ourselves the difference between *who* and *whom*. We knew what an adverb was, and we knew where in a sentence it went, and why it went there. We were aware of dangling modifiers because we could see them, quite literally, dangling off the wrong line:

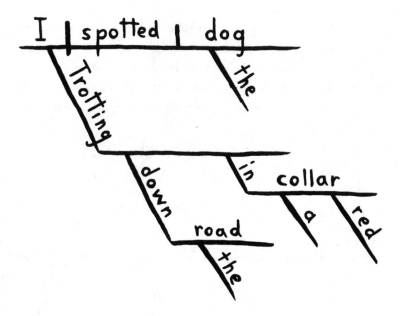

Trotting down the road in a red collar, I spotted the dog.

And we knew that gerunds looked like nouns but were really verbs because they could take a direct object:

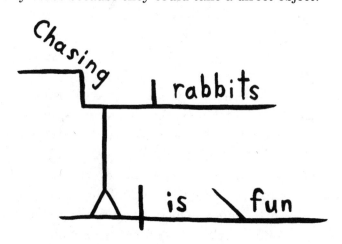

Part of the fun of diagramming sentences was that it didn't matter what they said. The dog could bark, chew gum, play chess—in the world of diagramming, sentences weren't about meaning so much as they were about subject, predicate, object, and their various dependents or modifiers. All you had to do was get the diagram right—the meaning was secondary. And for a bunch of eleven-and-twelve-year-olds, there was a certain wacky charm to that idea.

At my school, diagramming was part of our English classes for three years. Once the gates of elementary school slammed shut at the end of eighth grade, I never encountered diagramming again. Presumably, by then, our grammar was impeccable—a doubtful proposition, perhaps reflecting the optimism of the nuns about the perfectibility of human beings. With diagramming behind us, we were encouraged to use our skills in the writing of compositions on such topics as (I refer here to a yellowed copy of our school paper, which I was privileged to edit as a senior) keeping Christ in Christmas, the importance of good dental health[3], and why Nixon should be elected president, even though Kennedy was a Catholic.[4]

3 I won a prize for an essay on the subject that contains the somewhat startling—possibly ground-breaking—observation that "Good dental health and good mental health are related."

4 Answer? Nixon would be tougher on Communism.

*   *   *

The nuns, of course, didn't have a monopoly on teaching sentence-diagramming. If my parochial school education was quintessentially '50s (meaning regimented, bland, and conservative), the public schools were not much different.

My first exposure to diagramming was a year before Sister Bernadette presented us with her noisy dog. One of the few perks of going to my school was that, because Sister B. and her cohorts were Sisters of St. Joseph, March 19th—St. Joseph's Day—was a school holiday. No one else in the entire world got March 19th off—just kids who were taught by that particularly benevolent order of nuns. This was odd and wonderful, the equivalent of an obscure Jewish holiday like Shemini Atzereth. In New York City, the alternate-side-of-the-street parking rules are suspended on Shemini Atzereth; at St. John the Baptist Academy in Syracuse, New York, getting-up-early-for-school rules were suspended on March 19th. It was a day of strange, incongruous liberation. When I was in fifth grade, that meant I was free from the bizarre disciplinary practices of our teacher that year, Sister Agnella, who extorted a penny from anyone who dropped a pencil on the floor and two cents for talking in class—all coins shipped straight off to the missionaries in Africa.

So a day off was very nice except that, in the remote suburban neighborhood from which I was bused into the city to school, my few Catholic friends were citizens of schools not graced with Josephites but with Franciscans or some other order—all of them worthy, no doubt, but not, for some reason, as generous with their days off as the blessèd Sisters of St. Joseph. And my other friends—snootily known to us as "non-Catholics"—went to the local public school. So sometimes St. Joseph's Day, which in Syracuse is often wintry and bleak, could be, frankly, boring. Either that, or I was a hopeless nerd.

Whatever the case, on March 19th of my fifth-grade year, I went to school with my friend Carol Mae.

Carol Mae was a year ahead of me. Maybe a day in a sixth-grade class in a heathen school seemed pretty wild to someone like me, whose idea of a really exciting afternoon was reading *The Password to Larkspur Lane* for the tenth time. Carol Mae was my raciest friend, someone my parents considered distinctly iffy: her mother ate candy and watched the soaps all afternoon, their house was a cheerful mess, and her father was usually mysteriously absent. I was not, for example, allowed to go to Carol Mae's for sleepovers. Going to school with her, on the other hand, was considered a wholesome activity.

And so it was. I can't remember the name of the sixth-grade teacher at the Main Street Elementary School, but I do recall that she was strict—not wacky-strict like Sister Agnella but strict like teachers on TV: no-nonsense hands-on-hips what-do-you-think-you're-doing strict. I see her as tall and thin, with a name something like Miss Peckham. That may be a fantasy. But I do recall that, weirdly, she seemed to like having me in her class. I suppose the slight distraction was balanced by the flattering fact that I chose to spend my exotic day off under her authoritarian thumb.

I don't actually remember much about that day, but I do recall that the class was diagramming sentences and also "parsing" them, which we never did at my school but which I'm told was common (as diagramming was not) in British schools. Parsing involved shouting out the function of the words in the sentences Miss Peckham wrote on the blackboard—something like "The—article! Dog—noun! Barked—verb!" Maybe it was just a bad day at Main Street Elementary, but the whole thing seemed very boring and obvious, and I sat there thinking, no doubt, of my shelf of Nancy Drew books and wishing I'd stayed home like a normal person.

Or maybe Miss Peckham didn't have Sister Bernadette's flair. Maybe it was no fun without the element of competition with my peers. Or maybe it was like a training bra: I just wasn't ready. A year later I dove with glee into parsing's artier sibling, sentence diagramming.

* * *

5 And this despite the intriguing fact that *grammar* is an outgrowth of the word *glamour*: they are, in fact, the same word, through the magic of something called "dissimilation," in which glamour becomes grammar in much the same way peregrine becomes pilgrim. Whichever way you spell it, the word was originally about magic and witchcraft. Grammar meant learning, which a few centuries ago was understood to involve magic, or at least astrology. And even today, a glamorous person casts a spell.

While chasing rabbits may be fatiguing, and diagramming a sentence that says so may be rewarding, a generation or two later the whole topic has become, admittedly, distinctly unsexy.[5]

Maybe the world moves too fast to slow down for grammatical niceties; diagramming seems a perfect emblem of the earnest mid-19th-century times in which it was invented. Self-improvement in those days meant acquiring the trappings of gentility—and impeccable grammar was at the top of the list. (It was also the heyday of elocution lessons, elegant penmanship, posh etiquette, and ramrod-straight posture.)

People still hunger to improve themselves, but now much of it is about having flatter abs or better work habits or a more spiritual holistic evolved mindful outlook. There are no rap songs about sentence diagramming, no movies starring Meg Ryan as a pert English teacher trying to revive it, no true-crime novels about "The Diagram Killer" who carves I | am\ evil on his victims' chests. In a world of suddenly popular scold-fests like *Eats, Shoots & Leaves,* there are no best-selling editions of Reed and Kellogg's *Higher Lessons in English,* the ground-breaking little masterpiece that introduced sentence-diagramming to a grateful world. No one has illustrated it as Maira Kalman has so entertainingly *The Elements of Style.* On its back cover, *English Grammar for Dummies* even promises that "you won't have to diagram a single sentence."

I'm not really sure why what was mostly considered a lark half a century ago is considered dull today. Maybe now there are more larks in the average classroom than there were in Sister B's. But it's a sure bet that Bill Gates won't be adding MS-Diagrams to the Windows menu anytime soon.

chapter 2

TIMES CHANGE

Reed and Kellogg started the diagramming craze with their *Higher Lessons* (even the title exemplifies the period's air of dogged aspiration), but, in fact, they were preceded by a man named S. W. Clark, who in 1860 published a tome called *A Practical Grammar: in which Words, Phrases, and Sentences Are Classified According to their Offices and Their Various Relations to One Another*. Tellingly, the title page advertises that the book is "illustrated by a complete system of diagrams." What it doesn't mention is that the diagrams are balloons.

Clark was born in 1810 in Naples, New York, a town on Canandaigua Lake in what is now wine country. He was the son of a farmer but didn't seem to take to the land: he worked instead as a clerk in a store. Perhaps, even then, as he languished behind the counter selling potatoes or millinery or inkwells (the record is murky), he was pondering ways of making grammar visible. Whatever the case, at age 23 he finally quit his job and went on to Amherst College—graduating with honors—and devoted his life to teaching.

By 1860, he had been the principal of Cortland Academy in Homer, New York, for eight years. His first wife had died of consumption in 1849, and he had married Clarissa, his second, just a year later. And after testing his concepts on the captive student audience at the academy, and having been repeatedly "solicited" by the teachers there, he wrote the book that revolutionized the teaching of grammar and "with diffidence" submitted it for publication. Until then, parsing—identifying the grammatical function of the elements in a sentence, as in Miss Peckham's class—was the accepted way of teaching grammar. Not a lot of fun. But then along came Clark with his balloons!

With an edifying reference to Quintillian, Clark begins the book by comparing grammar to both geometry ("an abstract truth made tangible") and architecture ("like the foundation of a building… although out of sight and not always properly valued by those most interested in its condition").[6] He ends it with a strange little Appendix containing some orthographic trivia, the rules of capitalization, and a list of handy abbreviations like B.D. (Bachelor of Divinity) and L.S. (Place of the Seal[7]). But in between, Clark invented a system of crazy-looking constructions that look like those dachshunds fashioned from balloons at parties for toddlers—or elaborate systems of propane storage tanks—or possibly invading hordes of Goodyear blimps or giant hamburger rolls or, if you're in the right mood, a fleet of flying saucers. For Clark, the

6 Reaching for a simile a hundred years later, E.B. White likened grammar to baseball: "No ball game [is] anything but chaotic if it lacks a mound, a box, bases, and foul lines."

7 This has, alas, nothing to do with ice floes in the Arctic Ocean. It's from Latin—*locus sigilli*—and the term goes back to sealing-wax days when one's personal seal had to be affixed to a legal document.

sentence *Time slept on flowers and lent his glass to Hope*—whatever it may mean—was best visualized as:

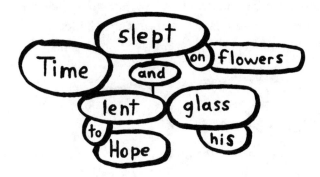

Clark asserts, "It is confidently believed that the Method of teaching Grammar herein suggested, is the true method." This was written before Strunk and White, among others, cautioned against the passive voice and the convoluted sentence—and probably the diffident Clark was too modest a man to come right out with a statement like "I confidently believe my method is the best." He was also thirty years too early for Twain's tongue-in-cheek advice—in his Fenimore Cooper essay—to "eschew surplusage." Clark goes on to say, in his preface to the fifteenth edition, "The diagrams are made to render the Analysis of Sentences more perspicuous," which I think means that the diagrams make it easier to analyze the sentences.

Despite his stilted prose, Clark has a poetic soul and is given to elaborate sentiments lifted from his vast store of learning. He provides wacky balloon versions of sentences like *The Lord uplifts his awful hand and chains you to the shore* and *Our proper bliss depends on what we blame* and *Satyrs and Sylvan Boys were seen Peeping from forth their alleys green.* (As I said, it doesn't matter what a sentence says, as long as it's diagrammable.) Clark also had a gloomy side: *The lame, the blind, and the aged repose in hospitals,* he reminds us—but, put into balloons, this idea looks quite cheerful. In fact, it looks hilarious.

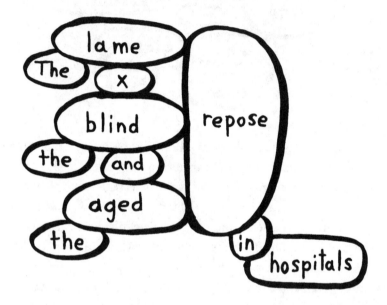

A few years later, Alonzo Reed and Brainerd Kellogg took the balloons and ran with them, but they straightened them out into lines and angles that were certainly easier to draw and maybe aroused less mirth in the classroom.

Both men were important pedagogues with plenty of experience trying to cram grammar into the heads of unenthusiastic students. When they wrote their book, Brainerd Kellogg was a professor at the Brooklyn Polytechnic Institute. He has a sober, respectable, impressively moustachioed face; it's easy to imagine him as a

Miss Peckham-ish stickler for not only proper English but good behavior. But he taught at the Poly for 39 years and was apparently a well-loved teacher. Kellogg was the very model of the high-minded, cultured, poetry-spouting, civic-minded professor. He was mentioned in the newspapers every couple of weeks for giving a reading of patriotic poems like "Barbara Fritchie" and "Paul Revere's Ride" at the YMCA, or supervising a debate at the Poly on the topic "Resolved: That Canada Should be Annexed to the US," or enlightening an overflow crowd at the Brooklyn Institute of Arts & Sciences (now the Brooklyn Museum of Art) on some highfalutin subject like "The Mission of Poetry" or "The English Language Philologically Considered." (If his nickname was "Brainy," it was apt indeed.) On the strength of his achievements, Kellogg was appointed to ever-higher positions at the Polytechnic: eventually, he would be elected president of the department of Philology (modern-day linguistics) and then elevated to dean.

By the time Brainy Kellogg retired from the institute in 1907, he was not only Dean of Faculty there, but also head of the departments of philology and English at the Brooklyn Institute of Arts & Sciences. He is memorialized fondly, facial hair and all, on the website of today's Polytechnic.

Brainerd "Brainy" Kellogg

His co-diagrammer, Alonzo Reed, apparently devoted his life to teaching (he became a teacher at age 16 in the little Catskills town where he was born) and writing grammar books. These included not only his landmark collaborations with Brainerd Kellogg (as far as I can figure out, the two of them wrote six books together), but also texts like *Reed's Word Lessons: A Complete Speller*

(1890), whose subtitle promises not only to teach spelling, pronunciation, and definitions of common words, but to "awaken new interest in the study of synonyms and of word-analysis." Reed also published a grammar book based on fables, among them "Two Wise Goats," which I found myself longing to read—goats are famous in pop legend not for being wise but for being wise guys, eating tin cans and other inappropriate objects—but about which I could find no information anywhere.

Reed's dedication to the cause of grammar, spelling, synonyms, and word analysis is especially admirable because he seems to have been a wealthy gentleman of leisure—or, at least, he lived like one. Whether his riches came from his grammar books or from another source is unknown, though a newspaper account of the time notes that Reed & Kellogg's books "have reached the enormous annual sale of about a half million copies." A copy sold for about fifty cents, so on an annual sale of $250,000, if Reed and Kellogg split a 10% royalty, each netted more than $10,000 a year per book—and multiplied by half a dozen books, that was a hefty income in those days. That figure, however, didn't include his real estate: Reed owned property in Brooklyn and a grand country estate, Seatuck Lodge, overlooking the water in what we now call the Hamptons. The house was so immense that after his death it was turned into a private club, and though his widow sold the place, she continued to live well, and donated an immense and grandiose bronze plaque in her husband's honor to the local Presbyterian Church where he had been an elder.

Alonzo Reed and his wife in front of Seatuck Lodge.

Alonzo Reed, at first glance, is an odd mix of a name—
one half Spanish or Italian, the other half about as solidly
Anglo-Saxon as you can get, like a shot of tequila on the
menu of a prim Boston tea shop. But amid the fashion of
the time for all things Greek and Roman—in everything
from architecture to hair-dos to rhetorical styles to city
names like Rome, Troy, and Ithaca in upstate New York
(including my own nearby Syracuse)—exotic-sounding
monikers came into vogue, especially for boys, displacing
some of the stolid Johns and Williams. Names like Alonzo
were far from rare: amazingly enough, Brainerd Kellogg's
own brother was named Sylvester Alonzo!

I've often wondered how Reed and Kellogg became
acquainted, and how they decided to collaborate on their
books. Knowing the coincidence of the two names provides
a break in the cloud of unknowing. I imagine Reed and
Kellogg encountering each other for the first time, one of
those historic meetings when the heavens shook. Where it
took place is irrelevant: a faculty meeting (Reed taught at
the Poly for seventeen years before retiring to his country
estate), a *thé dansant* to which they were dragged by
their wives, a lecture given on, say, Emerson and the
Transcendentalists—a hot topic of the day. They are introduced: Mr. Alonzo Reed, meet Professor Brainerd Kellogg.

> "How do you do, sir."
> "How do you do. Fascinating lecture,
> was it not? And—I say, my good man—I can't
> help but find the coincidence interesting in
> an Emersonian sense—meaning, of course,

in its transcendental aspect, the notion that
it goes beyond the conventions of reality as
we experience it—that your name is the same
as that of my esteemed younger brother, who
was christened Sylvester Alonzo Kellogg,
but who—perhaps understandably, considering
the nobility of that particular praenomen—
prefers to be known as Alonzo."

"A beguiling fact indeed, Professor Kellogg!
For, while I am aware that this goodly earth
does in fact bear its fair share of Alonzos, it is
perennially a delight to me when I actually
encounter one—or, I should say, so long as we
are speaking transcendentally—when I
encounter a fraternal connection to one."

(Laughter, followed by a couple of drinks,
followed by—yes!—*Higher Lessons in English*
and all its progeny.)

In their book, the authors give generous credit to
their fellow instructors: like Clark's balloons, the
diagrams apparently grew out of the suggestions of their
colleagues at the Poly. It's entertaining to imagine
animated debates in the faculty rooms at these places
about where to place the various parts of speech and
what on earth to do about interjections. Whoever came
up with the slanting line that indicates a predicate noun
or adjective should be immortalized:

He | was \ brilliant

And, as for interjections, here are a few of their gloomy examples:

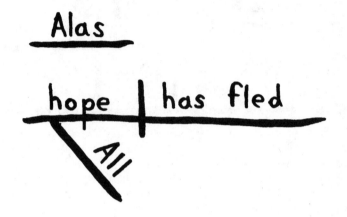

Alas! All hope has fled.

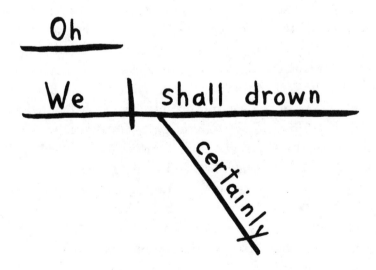

Oh! We shall certainly drown.

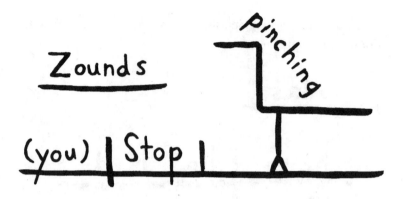

Zounds! Stop pinching!

Thanks to the wonders of eBay, I have before me not only Clark's pioneering volume (on which some bored student has done a perfect rubbing of a 1932 Indian Head penny in the back, just after the Appendix), but also a well-thumbed version (there were many) of the Reed-Kellogg book, a pretty little *Revised Edition*, in a size that would fit handily into a pocket.

The book is of its time in many ways, from its fancy cloth cover and a section on letter-writing printed in elegant 19th-century calligraphy, to its suggestions for sentences to diagram. Like Clark's book, Reed and Kellogg's also sheds some light on the concerns and customs of the late nineteenth century, a time very different from our own—probably closer to life in the mid-1950s when Sister B's dog barked, though I don't know what her sixth graders would have thought of such sentences as

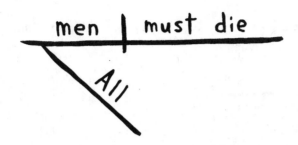

All men must die.

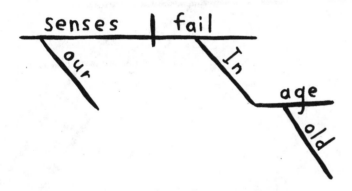

In old age our senses fail.

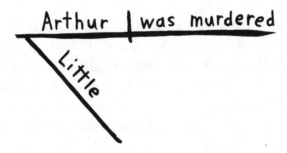

Little Arthur was murdered.

Or, my personal favorite, an Arab / Berber / Moroccan / Sanskrit proverb

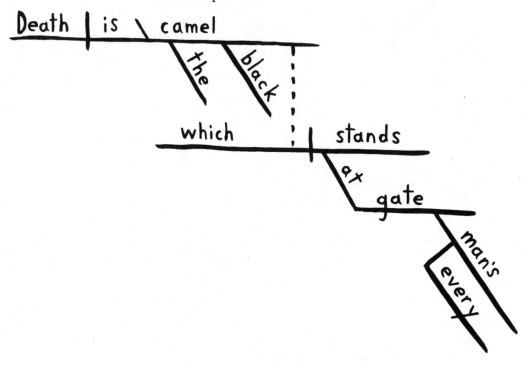

Death is the black camel which stands at every man's gate.

I suspect we would have been thrilled but a little shocked: at our school, we were as familiar with the Requiem Mass as we were with "Jingle Bells," but we had been taught to view death not as a camel but as a smiling asexual blonde angel who would lead us to our heavenly reward. At any rate, this kind of *memento mori* aimed at eleven-year-olds had pretty much gone out of fashion by the time I learned diagramming.

What's also worth noting is that, in a book designed for public-school students and written by two professors at the obviously secular Brooklyn Polytechnic Institute, the separation of church and state is glaringly overlooked. *Prayer leads the heart to God, and he always listens. I know that my Redeemer liveth. God tempers the wind to the shorn lamb. The immense quantity of matter in the universe presents a most striking display of Almighty power.*

Along with most other educators of the time (maybe arithmetic books were spared, though I somehow doubt it), Reed and Kellogg felt compelled to instruct students not only in grammar but in general knowledge—what we might call trivia. So their book is also full of interesting facts about, for example, nature. The "immense quantity of matter in the universe" included not only cats and dogs, who could be depended on for tame and down-home sentences à la Sister B, but much more exotic non-pets: *The toad spends the winter in a dormant state. The lion belongs to the cat tribe, but he cannot climb a tree. An ostrich outruns an Arab's horse.*

And Reed and Kellogg (or the guys around the faculty room coffee urn), though associated with an urban institute of higher learning, were not unacquainted with the simpler lives of farmers. In their book, the sheaves are gathered and the plough-boy plods homeward. They dip instructively into history, too, from the simple and incontrovertible subject/predicate/object kind of fact (*Caesar crossed the Rubicon* and, later, *Brutus stabbed Caesar*) to more complex sentences like:

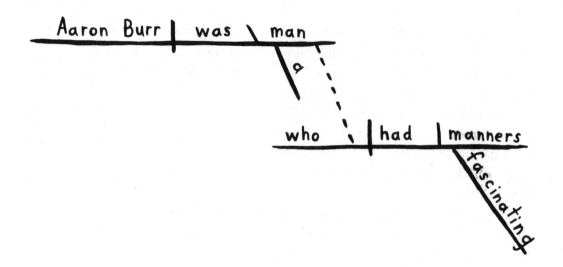

Aaron Burr was a man who
had fascinating manners.[8]

8   We were taught in school that he was a traitor and a murderer: his manners would seem beside the point. Maybe Reed and Kellogg were closet anti-Hamiltonians.

Nor were Reed and Kellogg above some statements that would not fly in a later age:

* *The Germans do their work with the most patience and deliberation.*

* *Alexandria, the capital of Lower Egypt, is an ill-looking city.*

* *He ran forward and kissed him.*

* *The laurels of the warrior must at all times be dyed in blood.*

* *The fairies were called together.*

These and other examples wouldn't be allowable today in a world where educators' exaggerated respect for the sensitivities of students has tried to plug up the juices of literature in favor of a dubious "political correctness."

Not only are words like "brotherhood" and "mankind" no longer to be found in textbooks or on standardized tests—maybe a case could be made for such excisions—but in one famous example, a reference to mountain climbing was eliminated from a test passage because test-takers who don't live near mountains might feel unjustly deprived and upset, and therefore be at a disadvantage on the test. In a paragraph about the ancient Sumerians, the fact that in 2000 B.C. or so they kept slaves was deleted. Handicaps can't be mentioned—and handicaps include chubbiness, foreign birth, gray hair, and living on a farm. And, needless to say, older people cannot under any circumstances walk with canes or sit in rocking chairs.

Reed and Kellogg lived in a more innocent, less self-conscious, more homogeneous time. They were cool enough, though, to anticipate the words of Bob Dylan in an illustration of the proper placement of an adverb:

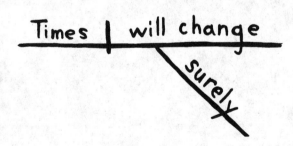

chapter 3

GENERAL RULES

Trying to stuff the complexities of the English language into flat visual structures is a bit like trying to force a cat into the carrier for a trip to the vet, and coming up with the idea in the first place seems comparable to the boldness and daring of cracking open the first oyster and deciding it looked like lunch. We'll never know what inspired Clark to pick up his quill pen and draw his set of balloons, but it's surprising that they were such a hit.

The balloons could be useful when they dealt with simple sentences: that barking dog looks comprehensible enough when he's turned into a balloon dog—it even has the look of an actual cartoon dachshund, albeit legless and with its tongue hanging out:

But when Clark needed to indicate a more complicated structure, he ran into trouble. His system allowed only for the adding of more soap bubbles, and more, and yet more—making for wheels-within-wheels drawings that require not only a degree of artistic skill but also the kind of mental capabilities that seem far beyond most pre-teens, even mid-nineteenth-century ones. Early in his book, Clark lays down the "General Rules" for diagrams, beginning with this:

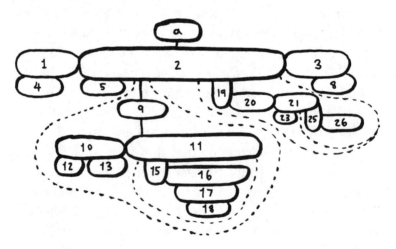

and moving on to the twelve rules for drawing them, of which Rule 7 is:

If the adjunct is a *Sentence*, it is attached by
a line to the Word which the Adjunct Sentence
limits; as, the Adjunct Sentence within the
dotted line (6), is attached by the line
from (2) to (9), A, and (6 to 19 inclusive) is
attached to (1), B.

Let's say the hapless student masters the rules and,
hunched over his slate in the Cortland Academy in
Homer, New York, or a one-room schoolhouse in
Centerville, Kansas, he's ready to draw some balloons.
Very soon, he's going to run into more trouble. Just one
page after he hits us with the rules, Clark offers this
easy-seeming sentence (cribbed from Sir Walter Scott):

I thank thee, Roderick, for the word.

Properly ballooned, it looks like this:

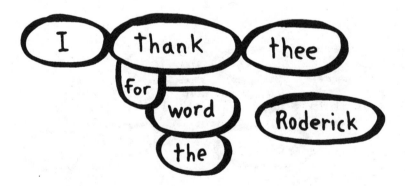

The trouble here is that it's impossible to tell from the
diagram whether the sentence should be read as Scott
wrote it, or as "I thank thee for the word Roderick"

(as opposed to the word Dilbert). It's a quandary that comes up regularly in Clark's brave and admirable book: once the parts of the sentence are transformed into zeppelins, confusion reigns:

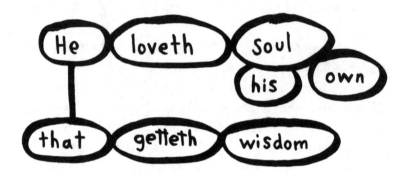

He that getteth wisdom loveth his own soul.

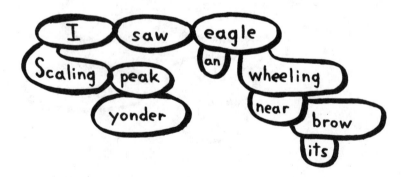

*Scaling yonder peak I saw an eagle
wheeling near its brow.*

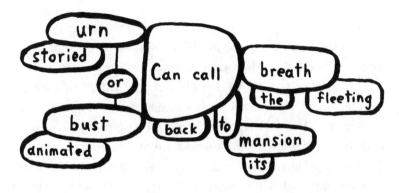

*Can storied urn or animated bust back to
its mansion call the fleeting breath?*

To which our scholarly young friend with the chalk and the slate might respond, "Huh?"

By comparison, Reed and Kellogg are models of clarity. Those twenty-plus years between *A Practical Grammar* and *Higher Lessons in English* were the Dark Ages of diagramming, during which an entire generation of schoolchildren sweated over bloated ovoids filled with quotations from the masters. When Reed and Kellogg transformed the blimps into roadmaps, life must have improved enormously.

When it works, their system is actually quite ingenious. From Clark, they got the general idea and even a few details, like the use of dotted lines as connectors (though, frankly, it's not always easy to figure out what Clark's dots were precisely for). But many of the refinements that Clark sorely needed are all there in *Higher Lessons*—and the switch from freakish balloons to sober geometric lines imparts a certain dignity to the whole process.

Reed and Kellogg began with a straight line: the expressway on which the sentence's most important elements ran as smoothly as a Jaguar tooling along Route 80. Lines slanting above or below it like side roads were for modifiers and connectors—connectors that could lead to, say, another sentence (making a compound) or a second clause or a modifying phrase, all of which drove along their own little avenues. For participles, Reed and Kellogg cleverly devised a line with an angle in it, which they explain indicates that the word is partly an adjective (which travels on a slanted line) and partly a verb (a straight line):

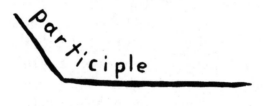

The gerund gets yet another kink in its line so that it seems to fall clumsily downstairs, which may be appropriate for a verbal noun:

They devised a series of steps for adverbs and adjectives that modify each other:

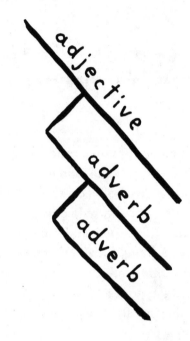

They use multi-story edifices for compound nouns, plus the broken line for coordinating conjunctions:

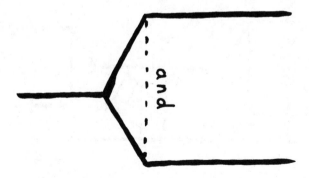

And they quite sensibly use a simple parenthesis to show an appositive—in this example, a noun:

noun (appositive)

As a sentence gets more and more convoluted, diagramming has to become increasingly inventive—hence the pedestal, a kind of access road for phrases that function as a noun or an adjective, or clauses that function as nouns. The pedestal may look precarious sometimes, with its huge, unwieldy load of words, but it lets you loft those monsters into places that are usually reserved for single units—like one of those huge, many-holed birdhouses for purple martins that you see stuck up on a pole:

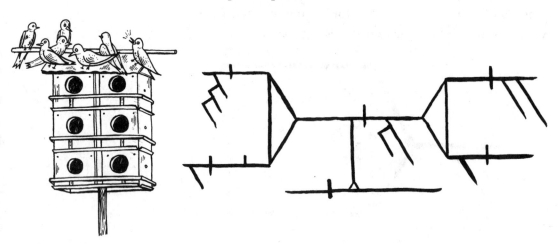

Diagramming also has its mystical side: it allows for the representation of something that isn't there. If a word is missing from the sentence but is necessary for its meaning, an "x" is usually the all-purpose stand-in.[9] In the example below, what is meant is that the house was more complicated than *the house* the birds had expected.

9 As we've seen, Sister Bernadette perhaps eccentrically preferred "(you)" instead of "x" when, for example, commanding her dog to stop barking. But in other diagramming situations, I seem to recall that she inflicted the occasional "x" on us.

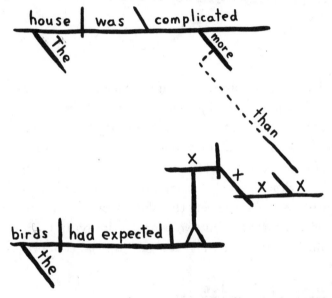

And, as we have seen, Reed and Kellogg, in their infinite wisdom, even came up with the dramatically unmoored floating line for direct address (*Mildred! Stop barking!*) or interjections (*Sheesh! Will that dog ever stop barking at those birds?*)

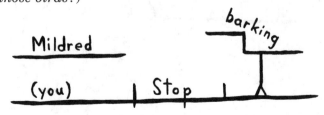

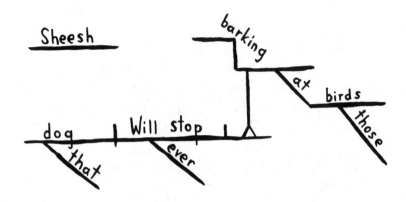

This complex system of highways and avenues became clearer when they chopped it into sections with small vertical lines, straight or slanting, cutting through the main lines or sitting on them like telephone poles. These divisions are eloquent in their simplicity: the aggressive slash dividing subject from predicate, the gentler one before the direct object, the slant forward or back as a subtle commentary on two words' relation to each other, the broken lines for those less substantial connectors.

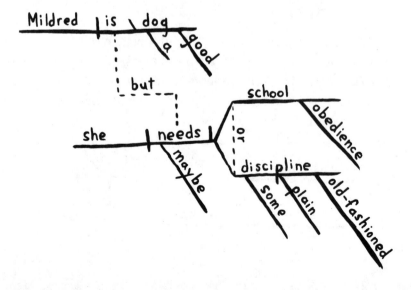

All this is still in use today, virtually unchanged. [10]

But Reed and Kellogg, like Clark, didn't allow for a certain awkwardness that seems built into the language. When the sentence gets fancy—not Henry James-fancy, just regular-fancy—there is no way to avoid an ungainly diagram that can confuse rather than clarify. Reed and Kellogg face this objection head-on in the preface to *Higher Lessons*, arguing that it's not a flaw but a merit, "for it teaches the pupil to look through the literary order and discover the logical order," forcing "a most searching examination of the sentence." But surely it should be possible to work backwards, deducing the sense of the sentence from its diagram: just begin with the capitalized word and follow it along its line from west to east, tracing its north and south byways down to the last little prepositional phrase. But this is often impossible, and because you can't keep the diagrammed parts together in a coherent way, the sentence emerges from its system of orderly lines no more clearly than from a fistful of balloons:

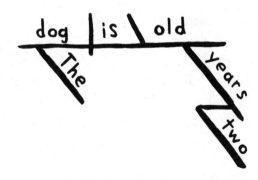

The dog is two years old.

10 In 1950, Homer C. House and Susan Emolyn Harman introduced an expanded system, and the book was a best-seller.

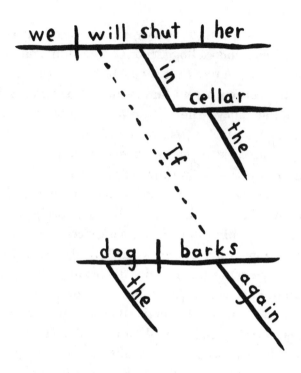

If the dog barks again,
we will shut her in the cellar.

These sentences, plain enough before they're Reed-and-Kelloggized, start to lose meaning when they set off down the road. (The dog is old? Oh—wait—she's only two. And you're going to shut her in the cellar? Ah, I see—only if she keeps barking.) The diagram can go only so far to accommodate their modest eccentricities; instead, they have to forfeit their character to accommodate the diagram. The more complex a sentence gets, the murkier it becomes when diagrammed—as we shall see in Chapter Four. It gets dissected, its parts get labeled, and then the whole thing is left stalled out on Route 84, waiting in vain for a tow truck—an exercise that has its uses, as we have seen, but that is basically pro-diagram and anti-sentence.

*   *   *

Diagrams have other limitations.

Reed and Kellogg, Sister Bernadette, and in fact several generations of English teachers have argued that diagramming sentences improves one's writing. The diagram, then, would seem to be the supreme test: launching a bad sentence on the Sea of Reed and Kellogg would instantly expose it as bogus. But the sad fact is that many substandard sentences can be diagrammed. And there are other linguistic evils besides bad grammar.

As I recall, Sister Bernadette never had us diagram ungrammatical sentences. (It would have been fun, but probably as risky as allowing us to go to a service in a non-Catholic church, which was strictly forbidden because, I have to assume, it was feared that we might like it there, and defect.) And in grammar books of Reed and Kellogg's day, there was no allowance for anything but standard English. The professors had no patience with colloquialisms, dialect, slang, or other nasty bits that got in the way of grandiose sentences like "Poverty and obscurity oppress him who thinks that they are oppressive" and "Every day and each hour bring their portion of duty."[11] They seemed to take delight in providing plenty of specimens of what they considered unacceptable English. In Reed's classroom, there was no getting away

11 I'm betting that some arcane but now defunct rule governed the use of *every* and *each* in this example.

12 *Huckleberry Finn* is banned today
in many places because it's
politically incorrect; in the 1880s,
when the book came out, it
was banned by the Concord,
Massachusetts, library for
"systemic use of bad grammar
and an employment of rough,
coarse, inelegant expressions."

with colorful outbursts like "That stupid fellow set down on my new hat," and Kellogg would certainly have flunked a student who wrote, "'Tain't so bad as you think."[12]

According to *Higher Lessons*, the sentence "I, Henry, and you have been chosen" is incorrect not because it sounds demented or because it could be misconstrued as being spoken by someone named Henry to an unnamed other (or by the unnamed other to Henry), but because "Politeness requires that you should mention the one spoken to, first; the one spoken of, next; and yourself, last." And the trouble with "I have got that book at home" is, somewhat confusingly, that "*have*, alone, asserts possession; *got*, used in the sense of obtained, is correct; as, I have just got the book." So in 1878 anyone who asked a Brooklyn Polytechnic professor, "Have you got time to help me?" would have just got himself into some big trouble. If you look deeply into *Higher Lessons in English*, there seems to have been some cockamamie rule in the way of nearly everything anyone might want to utter.

Standard English is, of course, the version of the language that has resulted from years of hand-wringing about the speed with which it has changed. But to try to hold back language change is like trying, as *Monty Python and the Holy Grail* would have it, to cut down the largest tree in the forest with a herring. The tree will keep growing. It's the herring that will perish. Spoken Standard English is now a minority dialect—maybe it always has been. Despite the best efforts of editors, purists, and Sister Bernadette, people go on "speaking English any way they like" (to quote *My Fair Lady*'s Henry Higgins once again), and writing it that way, too. Henry trained Eliza Doolittle out of her Cockney dialect and low-class vocabulary, but Eliza's counterparts today would raise Henry's eyebrows to unprecedented heights—and they don't have Eliza's incentive (room and board and really fabulous new clothes) to clean up their English. For many English-speakers, perhaps a majority, constructions like "Me and him went out" and "Mom laid down on the bed" are perfectly acceptable—not just in speech but in writing.

And they can easily be diagrammed.

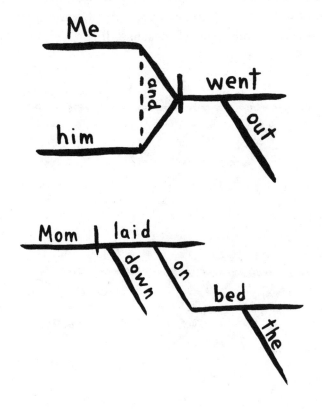

Both of those sentences are completely logical from the point of view of the speaker—and both are completely wrong. The diagrams alone tell us nothing about their wrongness: that would require a further explanation by the teacher. So what's the point? This can't be what Reed and Kellogg had in mind when they suggested that diagramming a sentence "teaches the pupil to look through the literary order and discover the logical order."

Noam Chomsky has pointed out that nonsense can be perfectly grammatical. His own example is a sentence both nonsensical and improbable: "Colorless green ideas sleep furiously."[13] This is as easily diagrammed as a sentence that makes perfect sense, like "Wingless black crows fly clumsily."

13 People have argued against this sentence's improbableness, particularly insomniacs who are all too familiar with furious sleep, and clever souls who point out that ideas can indeed be "colorless," meaning bland, and "green," meaning naïve—in other words, ideas that are so dopey they might as well be asleep.

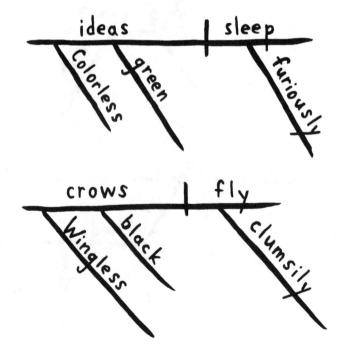

Or take one of those misleading and amusing newspaper headlines like SQUAD HELPS DOG BITE VICTIM,[14] which vividly illustrates the power of the hyphen. Even more splendidly ambiguous, because less easily fixed, is FARMER BILL DIES IN HOUSE. It diagrams like a dream, but that doesn't help us decide whether it's about a dead agriculturist or a piece of legislation.

14 A book of this title includes more than 100 pages of these groan-inducers.

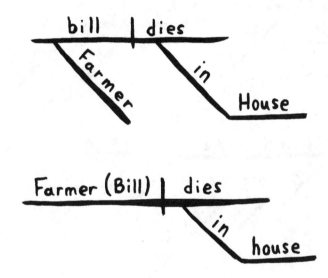

And Woody Allen, in his incomparably absurd essay "Slang Origins," as part of his explanation of where the word "fiddlesticks" comes from, provides this diagrammer's delight (I keep wanting to spell that "diagrammar"), which neatly illustrates a dependent clause, a couple of nice prepositional phrases, a compound object of a preposition, an infinitive phrase, and a hyphenated compound adjective:

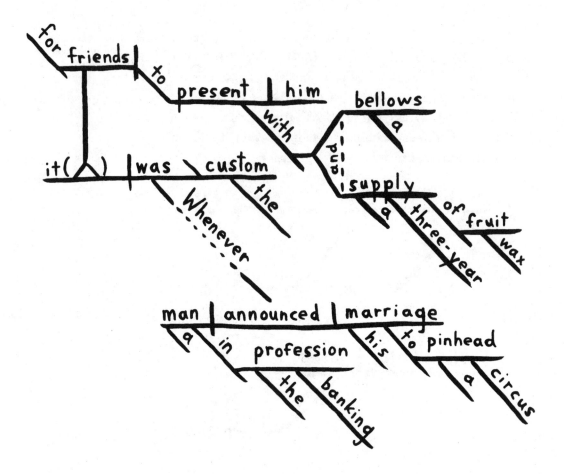

Whenever a man in the banking profession
announced his marriage to a circus pinhead,
it was the custom for friends to present him with
a bellows and a three-year supply of wax fruit.

Lewis Carroll's famously nonsensical "Jabberwocky" is also eminently diagrammable (and really fun to do), but the diagrams don't explicate it. Fortunately, Carroll does that for us in chapter VI of *Through the Looking Glass.* But knowing that *brillig* means 4:00 in the afternoon and that *toves* live on cheese and are something like badgers, something like lizards, and something like corkscrews, only increases its nonsensicalness.

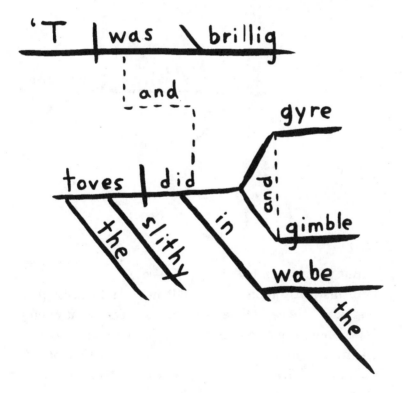

On the other hand, one my favorite sentences—supposedly a Groucho Marxism—is hell on wheels for parsers but is immediately clarified when it's diagrammed:

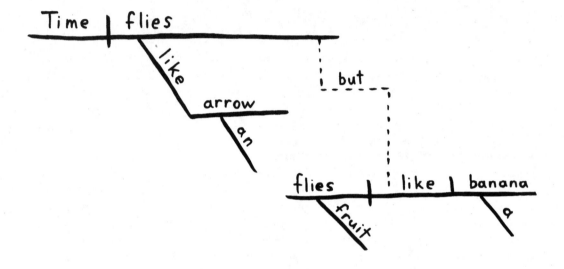

Time flies like an arrow,
but fruit flies like a banana.

But that is a rare and beautiful case.

In his justly famous essay "Politics and the English Language," George Orwell comments, "The great enemy of clear language is insincerity."[15] Despite the truth of this insight, the linguistic maven and conservative pundit William Safire has rated George W. Bush's hot-air-spewing second inauguration speech (known as the "freedom" speech because Bush used the words *freedom, free,* and

15 There was no way I could keep Orwell out of this!

liberty forty-nine times), as one of "the top 5 of the 20 second-inaugurals in our history." I've read the speech. It's lovely. But, unlike Safire, a lot of word-watchers, including Jacob Weisberg in his *Slate.com* column, "Bushism of the Week," find it instructive to deconstruct President Bush's more everyday English, which is usually mangled: statements like, "We want our teachers to be trained so they can meet the obligations, their obligations as teachers. We want them to know how to teach the science of reading in order to make sure there's not this kind of federal—federal cufflink."[16] (I could quote Orwell's essay yet another time, but I'd just be beating a dead tiepin.)

Like so many other bad sentences, the Bushism I just cited is baffling to the point of insanity,[17] but that doesn't mean it can't be diagrammed. Sister Bernadette would be tight-lipped and disapproving, offering up silent prayers for the speaker and perhaps for the country, but—after removing the halting stammers that are part of most people's speech—she could wedge those two sentences into neat diagrams.

16 George W. Bush, March 30, 2000, Milwaukee, Wisconsin.

17 As Twain would advise, "Use the right word, not its second cousin." Or its great aunt who is locked up in an asylum.

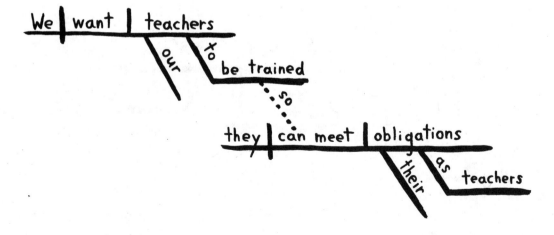

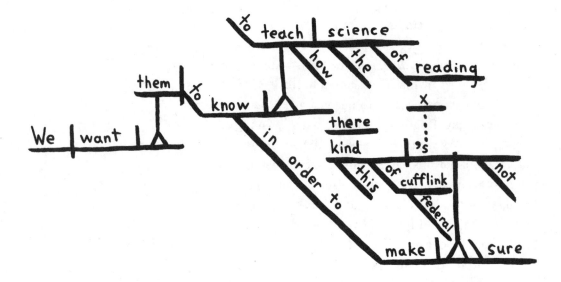

The substandard utterances I hear all the time on the streets and the subway, and that my school-teaching friends swear they get in writing ("Me and her axed him to take us to Mickey D's"), can also be diagrammed very handily.

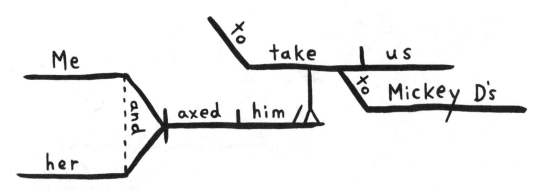

Axed in this context transcends its violent image and is simply a replacement for *asked*[18]—call it a synonym. It looks okay on its little predicate line, and if you didn't know it was "bad English" and saw it only as part of a diagram, you'd be like, what's the problem, dude? (The usage is not new: it was probably brought to America by settlers from the English Midlands, where it's still current. It's also worth noting that, in the first translation of the Bible into English (1526) by William Tyndale, *ax* is standard in sentences like: "And the people axed him, and sayde: What shall we do then?").

As for *me and her* in this context, who's to know they're not as good as *she and I*? Just set them down there on the subject line, where they look just fine if you never learned why they don't.

As I started to say a couple of digressions ago, although diagramming a sentence can sometimes expose its structural problems, it doesn't touch the deeper issues. A diagram can't ferret out a lie, correct a lapse in logic, or explain a foray into sheer lunacy. And, for all its tail-wagging cuteness, it can't expose the pitiful state of the speaker's education—or the problems with an educational system that cuts funding instead of providing our schools with smaller classes, enough textbooks, and well-stocked libraries.

18 I don't know why this is so widespread—and gaining. I used to think it was easier to pronounce. "I asked him" is, arguably, a mouthful: getting your tongue and teeth around sk/d/h is not that easy, and few people are willing to make all those sounds in a scrupulous way. It's more likely to be "I ask dim," the "k" sound amounting to little more than a tiny click, or—try it, you may find that this pronunciation in fact comes quite naturally—the much simpler "I assed him." To "ax" him is actually harder to articulate, and why it's so common, is a question that, as they say, goes beyond the scope of this inquiry.

chapter 4

POETRY & GRAMMAR

Gertrude Stein, of all people, was a big fan of diagramming. She's also probably the only major writer who has said so in print—and not only in print but in front of large audiences. In 1935, when she was nearly sixty and very famous, she sailed over from Paris for a lecture tour of the States, and one of the things she told her audiences was, "I really do not know that anything has ever been more exciting than diagramming sentences. I like the feeling the everlasting feeling of sentences as they diagram themselves."

Well, in most people's experience, sentences don't exactly diagram themselves; they have to be coaxed, if not rassled. But Gertrude Stein always meant what she said, and so we have to believe that, for her, those sentences marched along their intersecting lines like good little soldiers. In the 1880s, when she was in school in Oakland, California, diagramming was a recent invention. Reed & Kellogg's book was still fresh, teachers were probably still excited about it, and they passed that on to their students—the equivalent today might be a new reading program featuring hip-hop lyrics and biographies of sports figures.

I haven't read much Gertrude Stein. In fact, until recently, despite majoring in English in college and even acquiring an M.A. in literature, I am chagrined to admit I had read nothing of hers. I was dimly aware of "Rose is a rose is a rose."[19] And I saw the Rev. Al Carmines' Gertrude Stein musical, *In Circles,* in 1969 at the Cherry Lane Theater in New York, which should have tipped me off to her brilliance.[20] But it wasn't until I became intrigued by her comments on the excitement of diagramming sentences that I really discovered Gertrude Stein. I dipped a toe into her *Lectures in America.* To my astonishment, I found myself dipping another toe, then both feet, until before I knew it I was in up to my neck and flailing wildly as I struggled not to be sucked under by her astonishing prose.[21]

Everything I read fascinated me. Gertrude Stein sounds like a strange mix of James Joyce, George W. Bush, Lewis Carroll's White Knight, and the precocious three-year-old grandson of a friend of mine. And yet, like Carroll and Joyce and little Declan, she often makes a strange kind of sense. For example, "Complications make eventually for simplicity and therefore I have always liked dependent adverbial clauses." Or (and here

19 Gertrude Stein was fond enough of this pronouncement to state it in several different ways in her works, beginning with a comment about a woman named Rose— in her poem "Sacred Emily"— and going on later, in her American lectures, to state: "When I said 'A rose is a rose is a rose is a rose . . .' I made poetry and what did I do I caressed completely caressed and addressed a noun."

20 "Papa dozes, Mama blows her noses" has been lilting through my head for almost 40 years.

21 I agree with Hemingway, who said, after meeting her, "It was a vital day for me when I stumbled upon you."

she departs entirely from any resemblance to George W. Bush), "I have been very glad to have been wrong. It is sometimes a very hard thing to win myself to having been wrong about something. I do a great deal of suffering." And then, "We still have capitals and small letters and probably for some time we will go on having them but actually the tendency is always toward diminishing capitals and quite rightly because the feeling that goes with them is less and less of a feeling and so slowly and inevitably just as with horses capitals will have gone away." Her Theory of Diminishing Capitals is backed up by a reading of S. W. Clark's appendix to his *Practical Grammar*, where he stipulates that capitals must be used for "Common Nouns fully personified," e.g., "Here Strife and Faction rule the day." Like horses, indeed, this usage has galloped out of our world.

One of the reasons I'm so glad I read her thoughts on punctuation is that now I know that Gertrude Stein hates commas. "Commas are servile and have no life of their own," she says—in context it makes sense—and "what does a comma do, a comma does nothing but make easy a thing that if you like it enough is easy enough without the comma." And once you realize that her strange constructions are often (well, sometimes) perfectly ordinary constructions—just un-commafied ones—they seem almost normal (well, some of them). Armed with the knowledge that commas are slavish, enfeebling little suck-ups that are always "helping you along holding your coat for you and putting on your shoes," I found I could read her work with enjoyment—with, in fact, a kind of crazed delight.

22 "Don't call me Miss Stein," she once said. "Call me Gertrude Stein."

23 "Interesting" is one of Gertrude Stein's favorite words; she uses it over and over, reminding me of Humpty Dumpty in *Through the Looking Glass*: "When I make a word do a lot of work like that, I always pay it extra."

24 "It really does not make any difference who George Hugnet was," she tells us, but it does no harm to add here that he was a French surrealist poet, critic, and collagist (1906-1974). He and Gertrude Stein met in 1926 and were involved in a very intense friendship until 1930, when they collaborated on a book of poems. He wrote them in French, she translated them into English, and she apparently took liberties with his text, then demanded equal billing on the title page. Her response to the inevitable—and lifelong—rupture was *Before the Flowers of Friendship Faded Friendship Faded*—and there, a comma is useful but certainly detracts from the title's rhythmic perfection.

Gertrude Stein (it's impossible to call her either *Stein* or *Gertrude*, you have to say *Gertrude Stein*[22]) does use commas occasionally, but often they are substitutes for question marks (as in her remarks on the preceding page), because she loathes question marks even more than she loathes commas. "I could never bring myself to use a question mark," she writes. "I always found it positively revolting." Her revulsion is based on the question mark's appearance. It's okay, she says, as long as it's used as decoration or (weirdly) "as a brand on cattle," but "connected with writing it is completely entirely completely uninteresting." It's even less interesting than adjectives. Not only are they "not really and truly interesting,"[23] but also they aid and abet nouns, which are about as uninteresting as it's possible to be.

So what *is* interesting, Gertrude Stein, if you'll pardon the question mark?

Well, by 1935, in the talk on grammar that she gave to audiences around the U.S. on her triumphal lecture tour (and I have no doubt that they were slack-jawed and bug-eyed), she makes it clear that grammar is not only interesting, it's one of her enduring passions. The lecture in which she pours out her heart on the subject is entitled "Poetry and Grammar," but it's much more about grammar (well, sort of) than about poetry. Gertrude Stein, of course, wrote poetry (sort of) and in one of her poems (called "George Hugnet"),[24] she has this to say: "Grammar is as disappointed not is as grammar is as disappointed." (No, sorry, commas don't help with that one, actually.)

Some of her other pronouncements about grammar are more intelligible, some—believe me—less, but what really shines through this lecture is how very much she loves grammatical ideas, and how intensely she feels things grammatical, and how much she has thought about aspects of grammar that no one has ever thought about before. Gertrude Stein's thought processes are unlike anyone else's—except perhaps some of the characters in *Through the Looking Glass*—but to her they are crystal clear, and she is always definite in her ideas and implacable in her prejudices and vehement in her feelings. "One of the things that is a very interesting thing to know is how you are feeling inside you to the words that are coming out to be outside of you," she tells us on the essay's first page, and she comes back to this over and over: how do you *feel* about it, she keeps asking (sans question mark), like an obsessive therapist. "Do you always have the same kind of feeling in relation to the sounds as the words come out of you or do you not." Gertrude Stein, for example, has feelings about "the apostrophe for possession" and can see that "for some the possessive case apostrophe has a gentle tender insinuation that makes it very difficult to definitely decide to do without it." She, however, not being such a wimp, does do without it ("mostly," she qualifies) but admits that she turns to it now and then to indicate possession—as one might Google a long-lost lover—because she "has regrets."[25]

Has anyone else ever *ever* had this kind of relationship to a mark of punctuation? I myself have always had an intense partisanship toward the colon as a way to introduce

25 I wonder if Gertrude Stein would laugh at a satirical piece on the McSweeney's website, a parody of Strunk and White called "The Elements of Spam," by Jason Roeder. His advice: *Form the possessive of nouns by adding 's, just an apostrophe, just an s, a semicolon, a w, an ampersand, a 9, or anything.*

an elaboration or an explanation or a clarification, but it can't approach the passion of Gertrude Stein for periods: "Periods have a life of their own a necessity of their own a feeling of their own a time of their own. And that feeling that life that necessity that time can express itself in an infinite variety that is the reason I have always remained true to periods...." Heaven for Gertrude Stein would consist of cherubim and seraphim writing down verbs, prepositions, and articles followed by a firmly placed period—impossible in real life, but surely possible in heaven, or what's a heaven for? To stand by your favorite mark of punctuation, your favorite part of speech, is the mark of a true fanatic, a fierce *grammarista* who makes Sister Bernadette look like an amateur.

Who knows what Gertrude Stein would think of federal cufflinks or the death of Farmer Bill? But about, for example, sentences and paragraphs she is perfectly clear: "Sentences are not emotional but paragraphs are." And her entire writing life, she tells us, is devoted to trying to find a balance between those two. Sentences, of course, are what diagramming is all about, and when Gertrude Stein gets on that topic, all hell breaks loose. She gets revved up in her lecture on "The Making of *The Making of Americans*,"[26] where she states, "English grammar is interesting because it is so simple.[27] Once you really know how to diagram a sentence really know it, you know practically all you have to know about English grammar."

Despite her infatuation with grammatical traditions, some of Gertrude Stein's own writing may have been a sly, subversive construction of her own personal grammar—an

26 *The Making of Americans* is, perhaps, Gertrude Stein's magnum opus. Written in the first decade of the 20th century but not published until 1925, it is a long-winded, punctuation-free history of three generations of an American family—but anything less like the conventional multigenerational saga would be hard to imagine. As Gertrude Stein commented, "In *The Making of Americans* I was making a continuous present a continuous beginning again and again, the way they do in making automobiles...."

27 She asks, question mark-less, "So why make a fuss about it." And answers, comma-less, "However one does."

impulse that may be akin to her famous statement, "I like a view but I like to sit with my back turned to it." Turning her back on the Sister Bernadettes of the world, she became one of the few writers to construct completely undiagrammable sentences. What would Reed and Kellogg do with (from her novel *Lucy Church Amiably*) "He made many many tickle them as well as well as withstand"? How would Sister Bernadette tackle (from the play *Old and Old*) "The grass, the grass is a tall sudden calendar with oats with means, only with cages, only with colors and mounds and little blooms and countless happy eggs to stay away and eat, eat that"?

It's in "Poetry and Grammar" that Gertrude Stein tells us: "I really do not know that anything has ever been more exciting than diagramming sentences. I suppose other things may be more exciting to others when they are at school but to me undoubtedly when I was at school the really completely exciting thing was diagramming sentences and that has been to me ever since the one thing that has been completely exciting and completely completing." And why? Because when one is diagramming sentences, "one is completely possessing something and incidentally one's self."[28] Gertrude Stein always took it personally. Certainly Sister Bernadette never told us that diagramming sentences would lead to the possession of one's self—a concept that would have been only dimly comprehensible at my school back in 1955. She just told us that it would be part of our final grade.

Gertrude Stein and Sister Bernadette did have one thing in common. Both were obsessed with dogs.

28 In terms of paying for favorite words, she probably should give "completely" an extra five bucks, too.

29 As Dave Barry would say,
"I am not making this up."

However, Sister Bernadette was a very small nun teaching grammar, and her dog barked; Gertrude Stein was a very large poet writing books, and her dog sighed. In her grammar essay, she asks (no question mark), "Will you listen to one or two sentences where I did think I had done this thing" (i.e., balance the unemotional sentence with the emotional paragraph), and in her book called *How to Write*[29] she goes on to provide this example: "A dog which you have never had before has sighed." Anyone who has ever heard a dog sigh knows just how poignant it can be—and how much more poignant if it's a new dog, a dog you have never had before. What does it mean? Is it a sigh of longing for his old home? Or a sigh of contentment at being in a new one? Whatever the case, Gertrude Stein is exactly right: her sighing dog is both a sentence and a paragraph.

And, unlike most of her sentences, it can be neatly diagrammed.

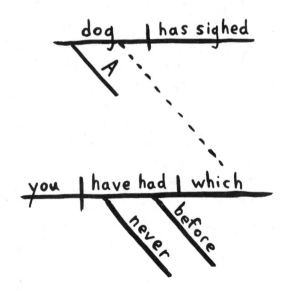

In fact, Gertrude Stein's thoughts about the unemotional sentence vs. the emotional paragraph lead directly back to her own dog, Basket.[30] On the subject, she tells us this: "I said I found this out first in listening to Basket my dog drinking. And anybody listening to any dog's drinking will see what I mean."

That's it. She doesn't elaborate. Commas don't help. Nothing helps. And yet her sincerity, her confidence in the rightness of what she's saying—in the *interestingness* of it—is absolute. And so is the utter mad uniqueness of her vision: who else has ever said such a thing, or thought it, or written it?

It's probably appropriate to end a discussion of Gertrude Stein with one of her short poems. It's called "A Dog," and it bears even less relation to a dog than her essay on Henry James does to Henry James, but it has a curious charm, and if we think of the invisible dog in the poem as an invisible sighing dog, perhaps we can feel its hot breath as we read:

A DOG

A little monkey goes like a donkey that means to say that means to say that more sighs last goes. Leave with it. A little monkey goes like a donkey.

And so leave with it we shall. But we shall not attempt to diagram it.

30 Both James Laughlin and Paul Bowles called it "that awful dog." There were several Baskets—she was hung up on the name—but the one everyone seems to remember was a large white standard poodle. Gertrude Stein said he was a great watch-dog "when he thinks about it," which he apparently did not often do, and had "blue eyes, a pink nose and white hair"—a "large unwieldy dog" who nonetheless was allowed to sit on his mistress's lap.

Gertrude Stein and one of the Baskets

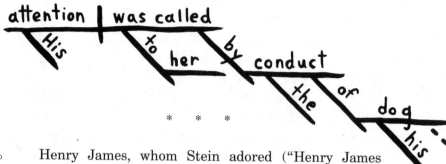

* * *

31 And according to James, the two
most beautiful words in the
English language were "summer
afternoon."

Henry James, whom Stein adored ("Henry James nobody has forgotten Henry James even if I have but I have not"), was perhaps the antithesis of Gertrude Stein. Or perhaps Hemingway (whom she also adored—for a while, anyway) was her antithesis. In any event, the two were definitely the antitheses of each other. James, whose style H. G. Wells famously described as that of "a magnificent but painful hippopotamus resolved at any cost upon picking up a pea," was the king of the orotund, elaborated, endlessly qualifying sentence, particularly in his later years when he compulsively revised his books, dictating them to a secretary and making them ever more dense, more detailed, more complex, more difficult. As Gore Vidal put it, James "believed that a work of art was never finished, merely abandoned." And, as James himself said in a letter to his niece (quoted by Leon Edel in his introduction to volume four of *The Letters of Henry James),* "I hate American simplicity. I glory in the piling up of complications of every sort." But James is underrated as a writer of accessible prose. For example, near the beginning of *The Portrait of a Lady,* during afternoon tea on the lawn of an English country house in "the perfect middle of a splendid summer afternoon,"[31] we find this delightfully Sister Bernadettish sentence:

His attention was called to her by the conduct of his dog, who had suddenly darted forward with a little volley of shrill barks, in which the note of welcome, however, was more sensible than that of defiance.

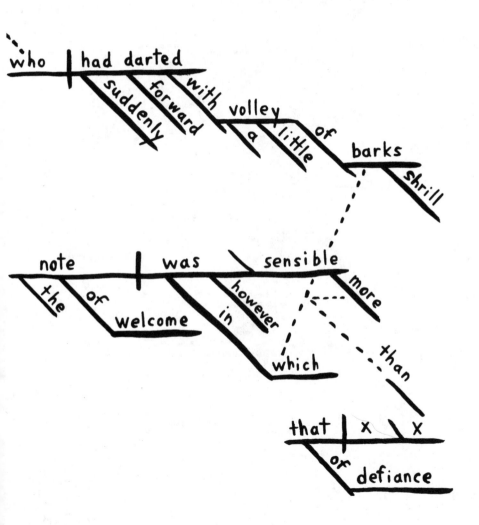

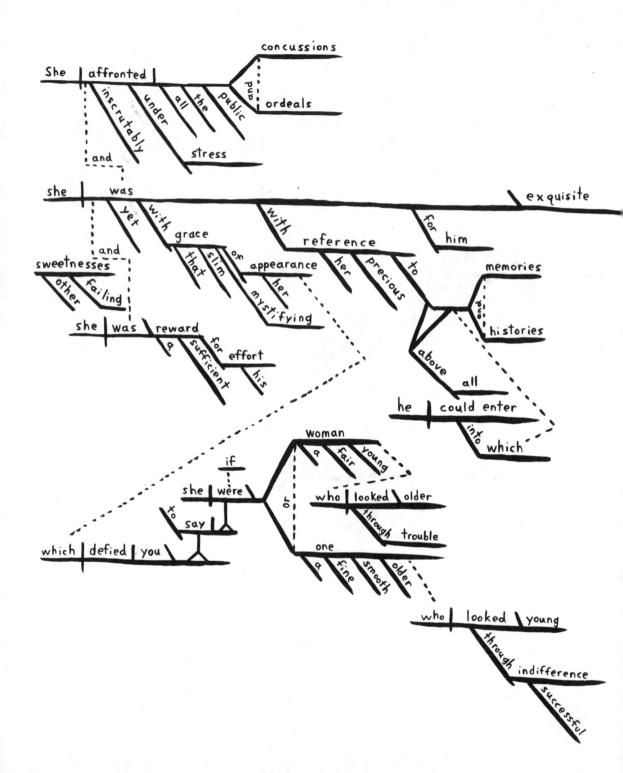

At his other, more elephantine extreme, James can construct convoluted but still perfectly lucid sentences like this one, from near the beginning of his long short story *The Jolly Corner*, one of his knottier works:

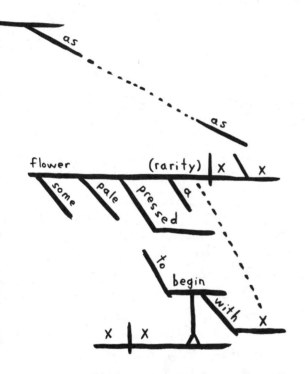

She affronted, inscrutably, under stress, all the public concussions and ordeals; and yet, with that slim mystifying grace of her appearance, which defied you to say if she were a fair young woman who looked older through trouble, or a fine smooth older one who looked young through successful indifference with her precious reference, above all, to memories and histories into which he could enter, she was as exquisite for him as some pale pressed flower (a rarity to begin with), and, failing other sweetnesses, she was a sufficient reward of his effort.

To which Hemingway might reply, as Jake Barnes did in *The Sun Also Rises*:

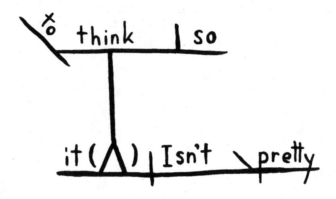

Isn't it pretty to think so?

James—a contemporary of Reed and Kellogg—was born in 1843 into a wealthy and cosmopolitan family in New York City, on Washington Square, and he learned English grammar (and French) from tutors in Geneva, London, Paris, Bologna, and Bonn long before diagramming was invented. Would learning diagramming have made his prose plainer, less intricate? His grammar is sometimes eccentric, he's occasionally difficult to decipher, and God knows his endless qualifications, delayed verbs, and freakish adverbial obsessions would have been greeted by Sister Bernadette with exasperation and possibly a rap on the knuckles. But Henry James, hippopotamus though he may be, is not someone to be tampered with by a chalk-wielding tyrant selling subject-verb agreement. Let him pick up his pea! And see how exquisite it is when you really examine it.

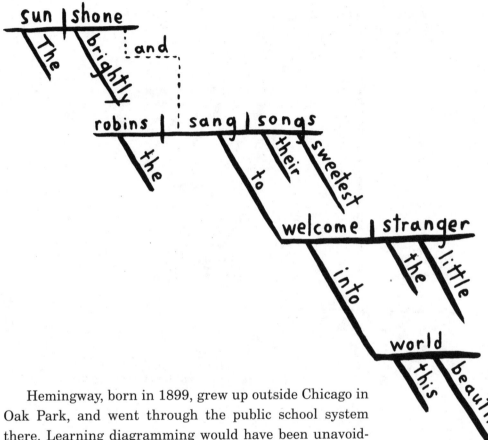

Hemingway, born in 1899, grew up outside Chicago in Oak Park, and went through the public school system there. Learning diagramming would have been unavoidable. If he was writing them then, his simple declarative (and readily diagrammable) sentences would probably have flummoxed his teachers, who were part of the Reed-Kellogg educational tradition that favored sentences that were as ornamented, embroidered, embellished, and frilled as the Victorian furniture of the era. His own mother wrote on the day of Ernest's birth: "The sun shone brightly and the robins sang their sweetest songs to welcome the little stranger into this beautiful world."

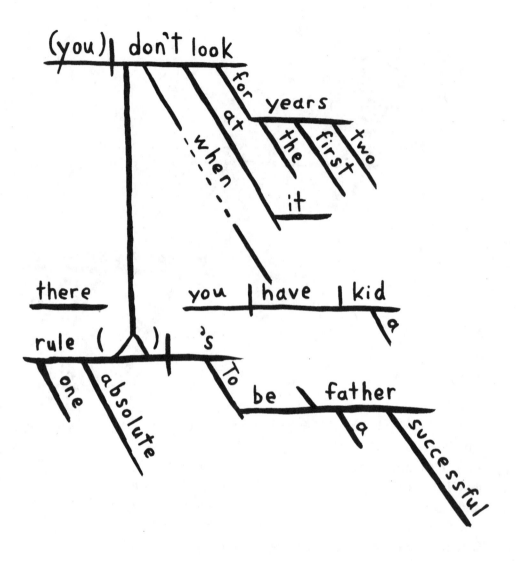

To be a successful father there's one absolute rule:
when you have a kid, don't look at it for the first two years.

(Ernest's own comment on the little strangers he fathered was "To be a successful father there's one absolute rule: when you have a kid, don't look at it for the first two years.")

Hemingway skipped college, left home as soon as he graduated from high school, and went to work as a newspaper reporter in Kansas City. He was there only six months before, in 1918, he signed on with the Red Cross as an ambulance driver in France, but it may have been at the *Kansas City Star* that the flowery prose of his upbringing was transformed into the vigorous, straightforward style that would characterize his writing thereafter. His letters home are casual, brisk, and colloquial, but—like most intelligent young people of the time who came from a public school education—he had a fastidious grasp of grammar that probably came naturally to him. It's doubtful he had time to labor over sentences like "Don't worry or cry or fret about my not being a good Christian" (in this possessive-plus-gerund construction, many people today would tend to write *me*, which is technically incorrect, for *my*) and "That was no idle Jest about the Great none other than that Mae Marsh, whom you and Sam glimpsed" (his *whom* is right on the money). These niceties were at his fingertips, thanks to the Oak Park schools. Diagramming would have been one aspect of a rigorous education in the finer points of the English language, but only one—in those days, impeccable grammar was taken for granted as the mark of an educated person.

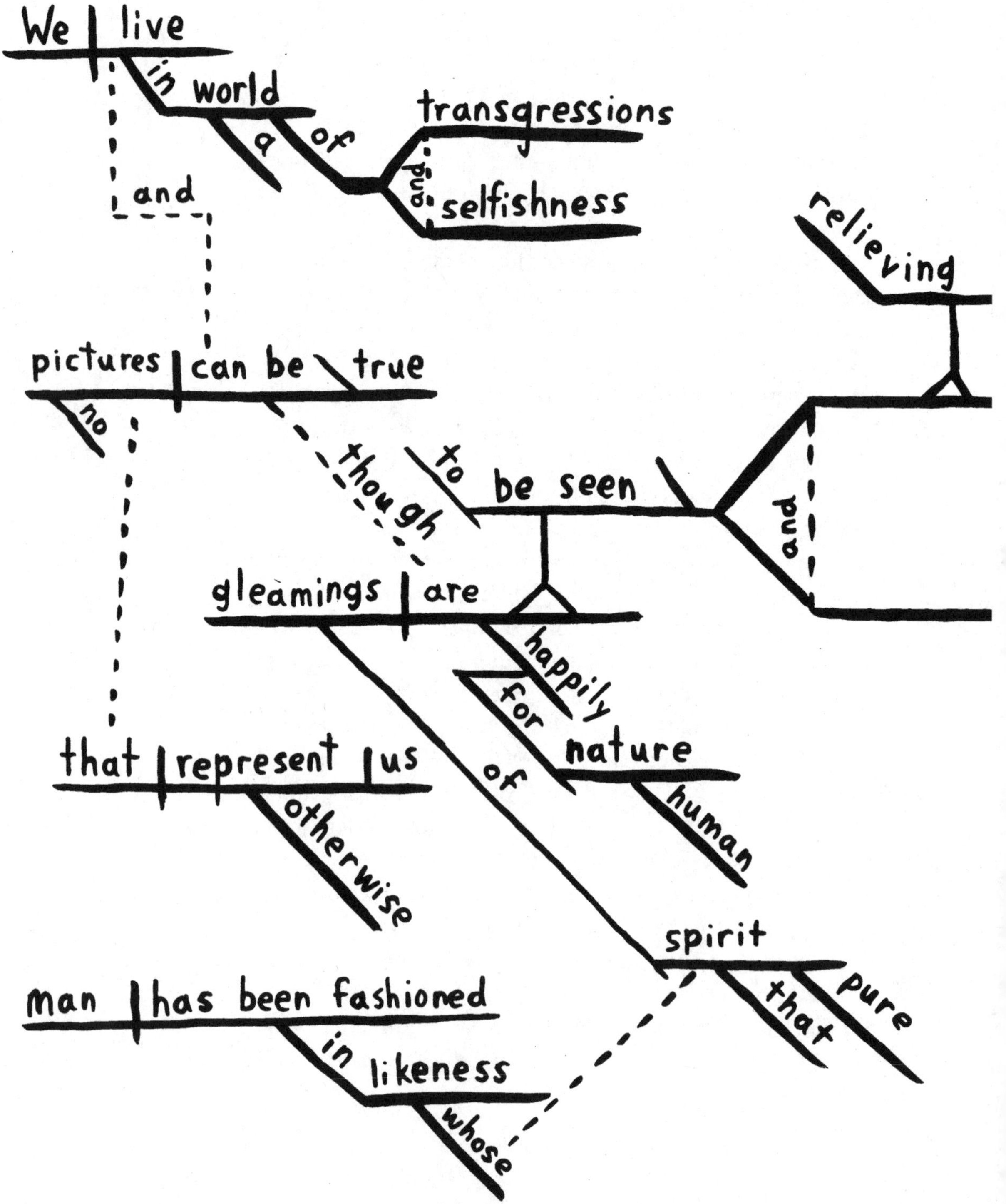

We live in a world of transgressions and selfishness

relieving

pictures can be true

no

though

to be seen

and

gleamings are

happily

for

nature

human

that represent us

otherwise

of

spirit

that

pure

man has been fashioned

in likeness

whose

As for James Fenimore Cooper, Mark Twain's avatar of all that was wrong with the literature of his day, here is the last sentence of *The Deerslayer*, published in 1841:

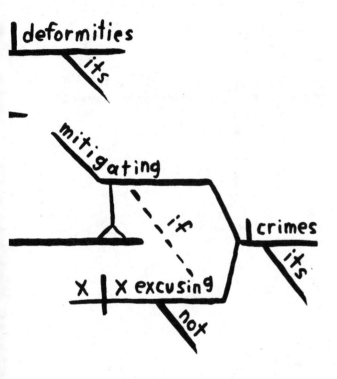

We live in a world of transgressions and selfishness, and no pictures that represent us otherwise can be true, though, happily, for human nature, gleamings of that pure spirit in whose likeness man has been fashioned are to be seen, relieving its deformities, and mitigating if not excusing its crimes.

And as Twain (speaking of antitheses) commented in
his essay:

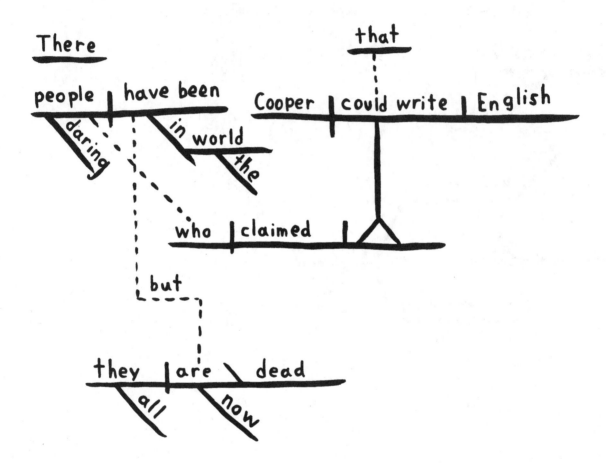

There have been daring people in the world who claimed
that Cooper could write English, but they are all dead now.

In Paris in the 1880s, Marcel Proust was spared diagramming at the Lycée Condorcet. Would a Sister B in his early life have simplified what developed into his famously complex sentence structures? Forced to diagram those baggy monsters at the blackboard, would young Marcel have slimmed them down? Proust is even more famous than James for long sentences[32], but in fact, he was equally capable of short, pithy ones. *A la Recherche de Temps Perdu* begins *très simplement*. The first sentence of *Swann's Way* (the Scott Moncrieff translation) is:

32 A poster that circulated in the '70s features a monumental diagram of what is said to be Proust's longest sentence: in translation, 958 words, from *Sodome et Gomorrhe*, the fourth volume of his magnum opus. My friend Sara Kane, on whose wall it prominently hangs, tells me that it is a sentence without a subject: "the descendants of the inhabitants of Sodom," the apparent subject, is displayed by the anonymous diagrammer in parentheses as "understood."

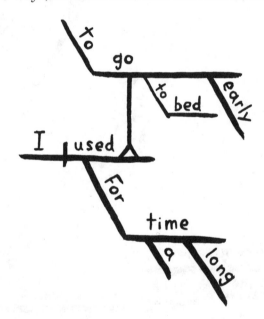

For a long time I used to go to bed early.

On the other hand, the final sentence of *Time Recaptured*—written ten years later, just before his death, is:

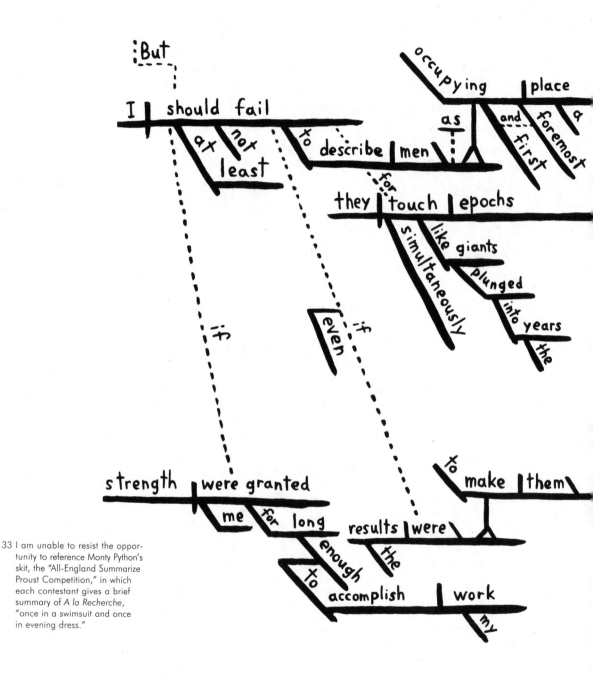

I am unable to resist the opportunity to reference Monty Python's skit, the "All-England Summarize Proust Competition," in which each contestant gives a brief summary of *A la Recherche*, "once in a swimsuit and once in evening dress."

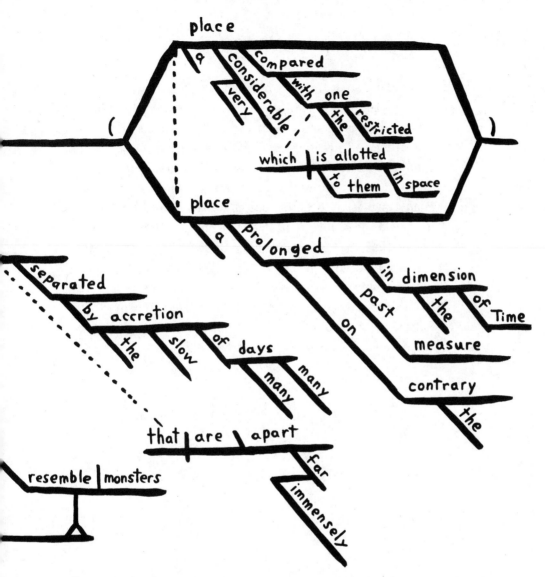

But at least, if strength were granted me for long enough to accomplish my work, I should not fail, even if the results were to make them resemble monsters, to describe men first and foremost as occupying a place, a very considerable place compared with the restricted one which is allotted to them in space, a place on the contrary prolonged past measure—for simultaneously, like giants plunged into the years, they touch epochs that are immensely far apart, separated by the slow accretion of many, many days—in the dimension of Time.[33]

34 The "Proust Questionnaire" is now
a regular feature in *Vanity Fair*,
which asks celebs to respond to it.

Playing a party game in which guests were asked to fill out questionnaires,[34] Marcel at thirteen answered the question, "What is your favorite occupation?" with "Reading, dreaming, and writing verse." He was not, perhaps, a prime candidate for the earthbound rigors of diagramming....

In fact, what's really tempting to wonder is whether such a sensitive, dreamy, eccentric boy would have been damaged by such ritualized pursuits. Maybe it was better that young Proust be slumped in his chair letting his mind wander, perhaps to concoct what, in the same questionnaire, he said was his idea of earthly happiness: "To live in contact with those I love, with the beauties of nature, with a quantity of books and music, and to have, within easy distance, a French theater."

Moving forward sixty or so years, and across the ocean to northwestern New York State in the late 1940s, we find Joyce Carol Oates having grammar drummed into her by Mrs. Dietz. In *The Faith of a Writer*, Oates describes the one-room schoolhouse where "We learned to 'diagram' sentences with the solemn precision of scientists articulating chemical equations"

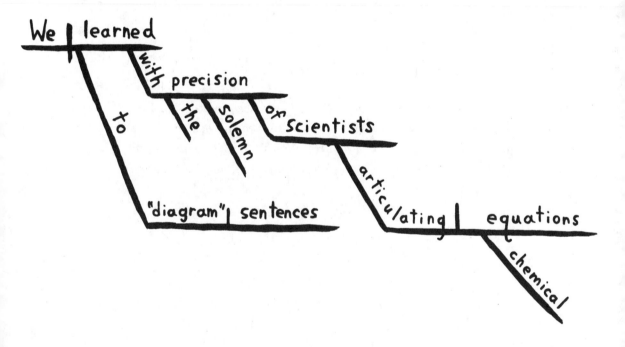

—and it paid off. Oates's writing tends to be pretty lucid—sometimes unnervingly so:

I secured his head in the clamp & now brought the ice pick (which I had sterilized on the hot plate) to his right eye as indicated in Dr. Freeman's diagram but when I inserted it through the bony orbit NO NAME freaked out struggling & screaming through the sponge & there was a gush of blood & I came.

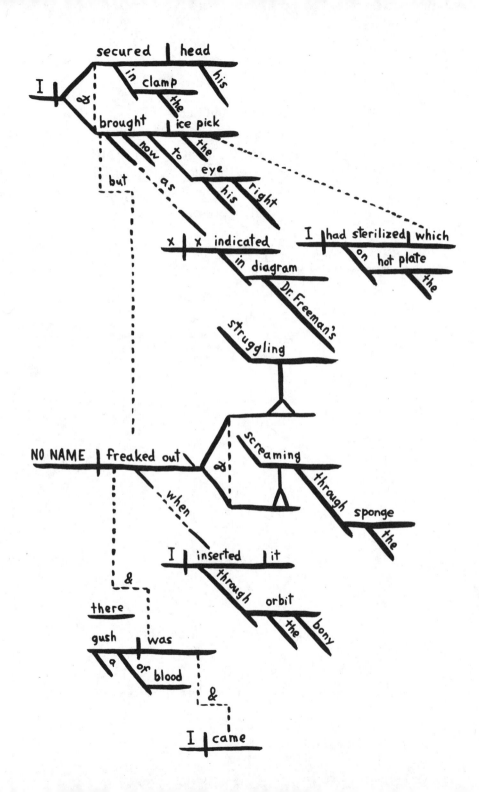

John Updike could hardly have escaped diagramming in Pennsylvania in the '30s. Amid the magisterial wealth of reminiscence he has committed to print, he doesn't say much about his schooldays, but he does describe his school's appearance—it sounds much like my own—in detailed, evocative prose:

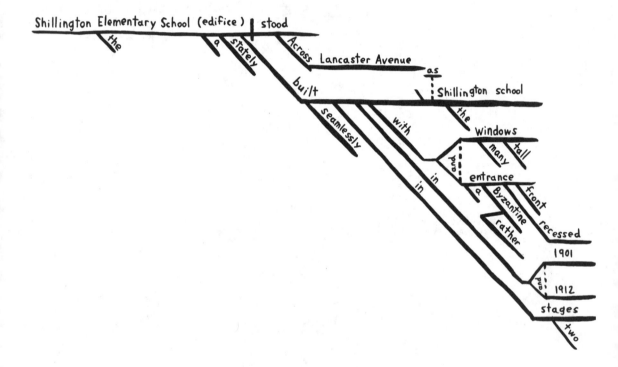

Across Lancaster Avenue stood the Shillington Elementary School, a stately edifice built seamlessly in two stages, in 1901 and 1912, as the Shillington School, with many tall windows and a rather Byzantine recessed front entrance.

Updike also recalls that he was an obedient student who loved school, and so we can assume that he was one of the champion diagrammers who marched fearlessly up to the blackboard, eager to demonstrate a grasp of the predicate nominative.

Thirty years or so before Sister Bernadette's dog barked at me in Syracuse, Jack Kerouac was growing up in Lowell, Massachusetts, a student at St. Louis Parochial School. (The school is still there, a red-brick fortress on Boisvert Street, but its most famous alumnus is not mentioned on its website.) As a precocious kid who was allowed to skip sixth grade, Kerouac might have missed out on learning diagramming from the good Sisters of the Assumption if the subject had been taught there. But that order of nuns was from Quebec, and the school served Lowell's French-Canadian community. Most of the teaching was in French—Kerouac's first language, which his family spoke at home. Diagramming was not part of the curriculum. Kerouac probably learned how to construct his astonishing sentences through his extensive reading: he haunted the local library, gobbling down everything he could get his hands on. (What would he think of the current school's assurance on its website that the Computer Lab has been upgraded "to provide students with the ability to surf the Internet safely"?) Some of Kerouac's sentences are lush, endless, twisting constructions—a diagrammer's nightmare—but even in their stream-of-consciousness meanderings they are perfectly grammatical, like this gorgeous portion of the final long, sad sentence of *On the Road*:

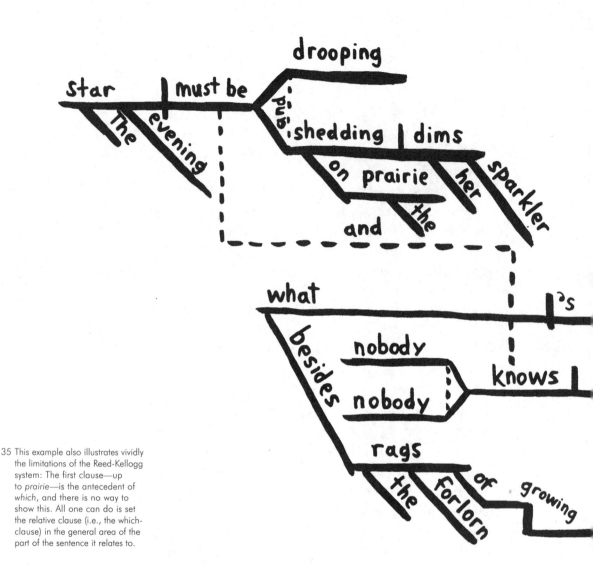

35 This example also illustrates vividly the limitations of the Reed-Kellogg system: The first clause—up to *prairie*—is the antecedent of *which*, and there is no way to show this. All one can do is set the relative clause (i.e., the which-clause) in the general area of the part of the sentence it relates to.

The evening star must be drooping and shedding her sparkler dims on the prairie, which is just before the coming of complete night that blesses the earth, darkens all rivers, cups the peaks and folds the final shore in, and nobody, nobody knows what's going to happen to anybody besides the forlorn rags of growing old....[35]

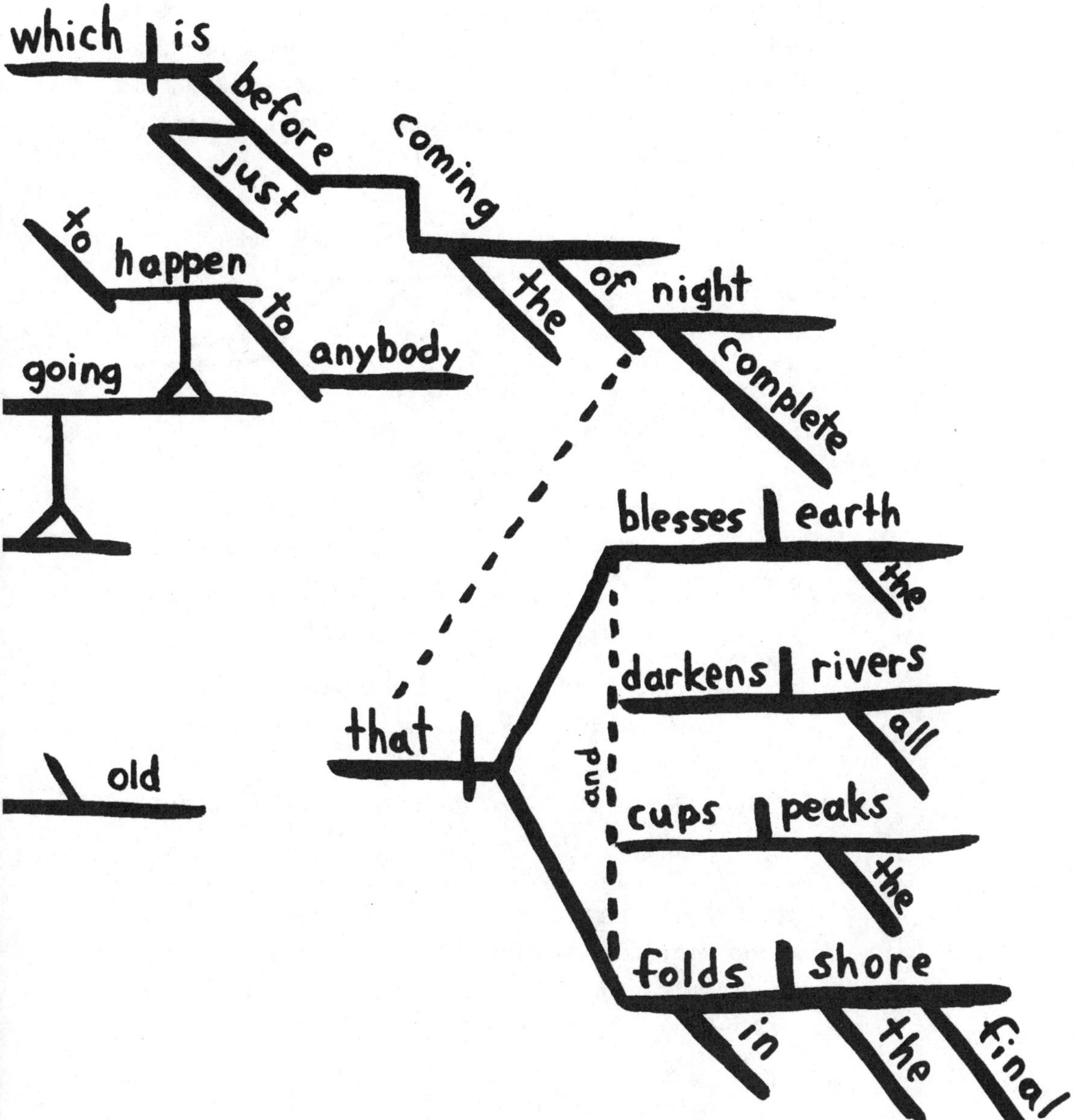
which
is
before
just
coming
the
of
night
complete
to
happen
to
anybody
going
old
that
blesses
earth
the
darkens
rivers
all
and
cups
peaks
the
folds
shore
in
the
final

F. Scott Fitzgerald was almost certainly taught diagramming at the private St. Paul Academy—upscale Anglo light-years away from Kerouac's working-class Catholic school—where he was enrolled from 1908 to 1911. Can we attribute the elegance of the last sentence of *The Great Gatsby*—

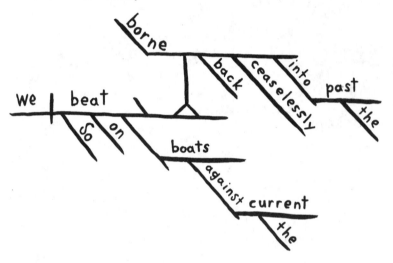

So we beat on, boats against the current,
borne back ceaselessly into the past.

—to some tweedy Minnesota professor? Did diagramming actually have an effect on the prose of anyone who was taught it? Are American writers from diagramming's heyday the writers they are because they learned to diagram sentences when they were kids? My guess is that they—*we*, since, my generation was the last to be steeped in it—were given a thorough, strict, daily grounding in the basics of English grammar, with or without diagramming, for most of the twelve years of their schooling, and that it stuck.

Maybe even the teaching of grammar is beside the
point in some cases. William Faulkner, writer of sometimes
obscure but undeniably powerful sentences, was surely
exposed to the joys of diagramming. But around the sixth
grade—that prime diagramming year—he began to get
bored with school (after years of incorrigible truancy, he
finally dropped out entirely in eleventh grade). If he was
taught diagramming, he may very well have responded by
gazing out the window and thinking about writing poetry
or going fishing. And yet—direct speech, which is often in
dialect, aside—Faulkner's grammar is impeccable, even
when he's inside the slow and uncomprehending mind of
Benjy in *The Sound and the Fury*:

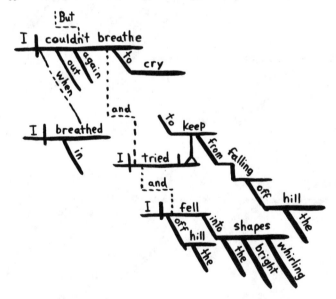

But when I breathed in, I couldn't breathe out again to cry,
and I tried to keep from falling off the hill and I fell
off the hill into the bright, whirling shapes.

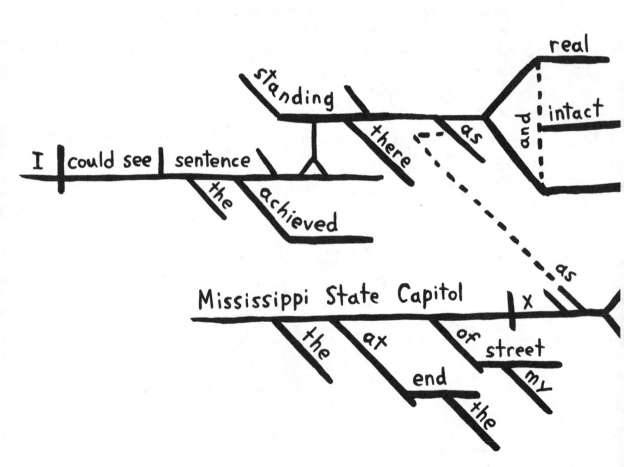

A hundred miles away and a few years later, Eudora Welty, that giant of American letters, was terrified into correct grammar by the stern teachers at the Jefferson Davis Grammar School in Jackson, Mississippi. In *One Writer's Beginnings*, she makes it clear that, while she may have learned to tell her *who*s from her *whom*s, she didn't learn to love and appreciate the intricacies of language until she got to high school and studied Latin, which made her understand "the beautiful, sober accretion of a sentence":

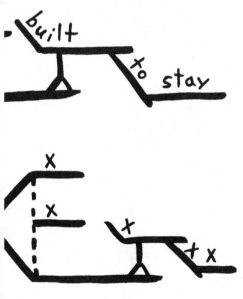

I could see the achieved sentence standing there, as real, intact, and built to stay as the Mississippi State Capitol at the end of my street.

36 Among her best novels are *Dance Night* (1930—her own favorite), and *The Locusts Have No King* (1948—mine).

Dawn Powell is one of the great (though to some extent unsung) American writers, a writer of wonderfully robust vernacular prose.[36] But though she was undoubtedly force-fed diagramming at her school in Mount Gilead, Ohio, she was a precocious but inattentive student, and ran away from home—and school—at thirteen to escape her evil stepmother and live with her aunt, who ran a boarding house where Dawn helped her aunt feed the guests. She eventually changed her mind about education, and graduated with honors from high school, where she was editor of the yearbook and capable of statements like this one from the diary she kept at the time:

I must make myself strong for the knocks that are to come, for no matter what you tell me something in me says that life for me holds more knocks than joys, and the blows will leave me crushed, stunned, wild-eyed and ready to die, while the joys will make me deliriously, wildly, gloriously happy.

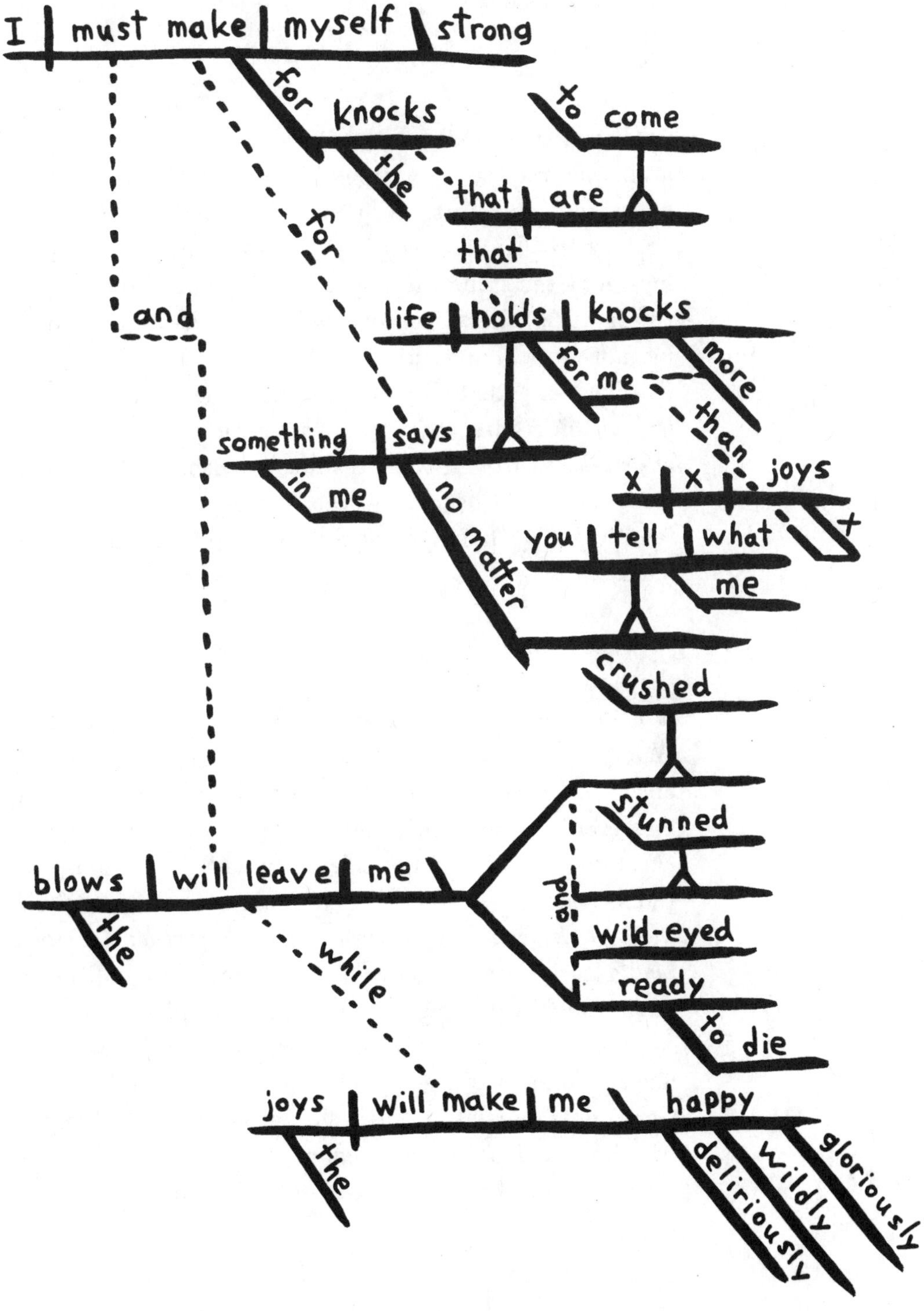
I
must make
myself
strong
for
knocks
the
to
come
that
are
that
life
holds
knocks
for
me
more
than
something
says
in
me
no matter
x
x
joys
x
you
tell
what
me
crushed
stunned
and
wild-eyed
ready
to
die
blows
will leave
me
the
while
joys
will make
me
happy
the
deliriously
wildly
gloriously

Few people would deny that students need to master grammar in order to write decently. But there are other places to acquire it than in sixth-grade grammar classes. And where brilliant writing "comes from" is always a mystery—the simple answer is that it comes from deep in the psyche of the writer who perpetrates it—but there's a lot more to it than correct grammar.

The fact is that a lot of people don't need diagramming or anything else: they pick up grammar and syntax effortlessly through their reading—which, in the case of most competent users of words, ranges from extensive to fanatical. The language sticks to them like cat hair to black trousers, and they do things correctly without knowing why.

Others understand their own language only when they study a foreign one: seeing it from the outside makes it come clear, particularly—as in the case of Eudora Welty—with the study of Latin, which is a bit like an encyclopedia of grammatical principles. Once you've mastered, for example, the elegantly succinct ablative absolute in Latin (and, incidentally, seen how clumsy its English equivalent can be: *With the dog barking furiously, the girl drew a diagram* versus *Cane fortiter latrante, puella descriptionem describat*), you probably will never have trouble with your own language again.

For many of the world's great literary writers, diagramming would seem to be seriously beside the point. Gertrude Stein, after all, was steeped in diagramming in school and clutched it happily to her bosom, but it didn't prevent her from writing like Gertrude Stein.

chapter 5

YOUSE AIN'T
GOT NO CLASS

The world's most famous—maybe *only* famous—copy editor was Eleanor Gould Packard, who worked in that capacity at *The New Yorker* for nearly 55 years and merited not only an admiring obituary in the *Times* but also a thank-you from E. B. White in *The Elements of Style*. She was known to sometimes go too far: one of her claims to fame was the finding of four grammatical errors in a three-word sentence.[37] As the magazine's longtime fiction editor, Roger Angell, has commented, if all her recommendations had been carried out, the magazine's famously lucent prose "would be like the purest water—absolutely tasteless." And yet she was revered for her abilities, and generations of *New Yorker* writers claimed that she was vital to the magazine's excellence.

I have not always been a copy editor. I've considered myself a writer since I was a kid and have been publishing

37 The sentence was perpetrated by *The New Yorker* staff writer Lawrence Weschler, but, unfortunately, no one recalls what it was.

fiction and essays for twenty-five years, but it was only a few years ago that I became a professional copy editor—i.e., someone who messes with other people's prose and gets paid for it. For me, transforming an *almost* good sentence into a *very* good sentence is a satisfaction equivalent to dipping strawberries into whipped cream.

The downside is that I can't relax: surrounded by English, much of it wandering to some degree from the path of linguistic perfection that meanders through my mind, I spot problems everywhere I look. I worked in a New Haven bookstore back in the '80s, and to this day I can't go into a Borders or a Joe's Book Shack without compulsively straightening the books on the shelves. And when I spot an error (like this egregious misspelling from—yes—*The New Yorker:* "[A]fter drinking it I wondered for several moments if I would wretch"[38]), my blood begins to boil, or at least come to a simmer you could poach an egg in.

I've often wished I could diagram a sentence to illustrate for its writer exactly what the problem is. Would it work? Meaning, would a diagram stanch the flow of dangling modifiers and *whom*lessness and *it's* confused with *its* in which the average person's writing is awash? Probably not. The diagram depends solely on its constructor's knowledge of grammar. Those intersecting lines always look just fine, but what's on them, as we have seen, could be flat-out wrong. The limitation of diagramming is that it's so limited! What distresses a good copy editor most, I think, is the failure of the prose to match the cogency of the ideas it's trying to express. People are often smart; writing is often dumb. But forcing people up to the blackboard with a piece of chalk isn't going to help much.

38 March 13, 2006, page 43. Eleanor Gould Packard retired in 1999.

Fortunately for me, the solution many people turn to is: hire an editor. But that requires a certain amount of humility. Language permeates our lives—it's crucial to nearly everything we do, from buying a shovel to sustaining a relationship, but it's something we've all been intimately connected with since we started babbling our *dadas* and *googoos*. It's not easy to admit that we're not as expert at it as we are at, say, walking and using the bathroom, which we were mastering around the same time that our language skills were kicking in. And, after all, everyone knows what you mean (to quote two recent sentences that came across my desk) when you write "She lost her mother as a child to cancer" or "Although believed to have been a suicide, the detective finds himself compelled to look deeper into the case." Or do they? Diagramming might help. But only if the writer has been given a solid grammatical training by a Miss Peckham, a Mrs. Dietz, or a Sister Bernadette.

Diagramming, of course, is only one of the more recent attempts to reform the English language, an objective that is far from new. It probably began with the invention of the printing press, which brought books to the masses and saw the beginnings of attempts to codify the big sloppy mess that was English. By the eighteenth century, dictionaries had been written, grammarians were being born, language snobs were rampant, and confusion continued to reign—as it does today. During its first many hundreds of years, as the language sorted itself out, it had been allowed to do anything it liked. *Who* and *whom* were interchangeable, *more better* was perfectly acceptable, and Shakespeare never really could decide how to spell his own name.

39 *I don't give a damn for a man that can only spell a word one way.* —Mark Twain

40 *When I split an infinitive, God damn it, I split it so it stays split.* —Raymond Chandler

(Shakspere? Shaksper? Shakspear? Schakspere?)[39] But eventually, the people who like things to be neat and tidy began to get on the case of people who just want to let it all hang out as long as they, like, express themselves. It was decreed that splitting infinitives[40] was a crime and that ending sentences with prepositions was something up with which we should not put. I love E. B. White's example, in a 1962 letter to his publisher, of a sentence that ends with five prepositions: "A father of a little boy goes upstairs after supper to read to his son, but he brings the wrong book. The boy says, 'What did you bring that book that I don't want to be read to out of up for?'" (On the other hand, when White—let's call him a stickler with a great sense of humor—asked his granddaughter when she was moving into her new apartment and she replied, "Hopefully, on Tuesday," he reports that he nearly choked on his lunch.)

It's an ongoing dilemma. How important is "correct" English? Isn't the important thing getting one's thoughts on paper? The process is not always easy, and maybe such considerations as subject-verb agreement and parallel construction are silly, irrelevant, artificial concerns that accomplish little and hinder much.

For anyone involved in the English language biz, it's impossible to entirely escape the dispute between the two schools of thought on the subject. There are the prescriptivists—sometimes called not only language snobs but grammar police, elitists, meanies, pedants, undersexed schoolmarms, racists, and worse—who go back far beyond not only Eleanor Gould Packard but also Kellogg and Reed.

The first English grammar book was published in 1586, and in 1712 Jonathan Swift proposed the creation of an English Academy, on the model of the French, to keep English pure and unsullied.[41] (The chief of the American language police, John Simon, resurrected this idea in his 1980 book *Paradigms Lost*.) The prescriptivists insist that there is a right way and a wrong way to speak and (especially) to write English, and that words like *finalize* and *prioritize* are fit only for bozos and barbarians.

And then there are the descriptivists. They came tripping out of the closet in 1961 with the publication of the ultra-permissive *Webster's Third International Dictionary*, which includes not only *finalize* (considered by purists to be bureaucratic gobbledegook)[42] but *irregardless* and *alright* because that's how people use them or spell them. For a descriptivist, as for an eighteenth-century Deist, "whatever is, is right"—sometimes shortened in our world to a plain "whatever."

Webster's Third was, needless to say, a red flag to the fuddiest of the duddies—the crowd that believes that dictionaries are there to instruct rather than to reflect current usage, that "bad English" is accompanied by loose morals,[43] and that people spoke better English (just as they listened to better music and fought better wars) back in the good old days. The two groups have been on the warpath ever since. In the March 1997 issue of *The Atlantic Monthly*, Mark Halpern (major prescriptivist), called it "a war that never ends," and each generation brings new ammunition. As David Crystal puts it, "One generation's linguistic pedant is the next generation's

41 No, it's not like *A Modest Proposal*. He was quite serious. In "A Proposal for Correcting, Improving, and Ascertaining the English Tongue," he blamed the degeneration of English on, among other things, "illiterate Court-Fops, half-witted Poets, and University-Boys." The Swifts of today—the most extreme of the prescriptivists—tend to blame it on TV, the permissive '60s, and a political correctness that supposedly caters to minorities.

42 The newest edition of *Webster's*—the Eleventh—notes, mildly, "It usually is not found in *belles-lettres*."

43 In *The Stories of English*, David Crystal finds it necessary to set the record straight: "There is no simple or direct relationship between grammar and behavior."

44 The chances are enormous that a certain percentage of people reading this sentence will take *butt* to refer to someone's backside—thus does the language grow and change.

critical butt."[44] Even Reed and Kellogg, in a sentence meant to illustrate a two-word predicate, acknowledged succinctly that

Grammarians | will differ

45 I was taught that the proper construction is "I am taller than he"—a short way of saying "I am taller than he is." This way, *I* and *he* are both in the same case, the nominative. Now that I think about it, this seems like irrational nitpicking, but I'm sticking with it anyway, as a little *hommage* to the Sister Bernadettes in my life.

46 In *Saturday,* Ian McEwan writes this sentence: "Distress is making him nauseous." I know it sounds Miss Peckhamish, but there's a nice distinction—rapidly disappearing—between *nauseous* (causing disgust) and *nauseated* (feeling disgust).

47 This must be related to the woefully mistaken belief that "penultimate" means "the absolute last," simply because it sounds as if that's what it should mean.

I'd have to describe myself as something like a medium-strength prescriptivist, or a situational semi-descriptivist, or maybe just a linguistic agnostic. When I'm not getting paid to do so, I do my best to keep a lid on my aversion to "I am taller than him"[45] and the use of "enormity" (which means "very great wickedness") to mean "very large hugeness." I don't go as far as the writer David Foster Wallace, who has written that "listening to most people's English feels like watching somebody use a Stradivarius to pound nails." But, like Strunk and White, I can't keep myself from deploring, for example, the substitution of "nauseous" for "nauseated," which surfaces in everything from the compositions of nine-year-olds to best-selling novels by Booker Prize-winners.[46] And I spend quite a bit of time sorting out "that" from "which" and putting in and removing hyphens and (something new and frightening I've begun to see lately) battling the idea that "infinitesimal" means not "very very small" but "endless."[47]

As someone who inhabits both roles, I must confess that I like editing my own work more than I do writing it. I find first drafts painful; what I love is to revise and polish. Sometimes I think I write simply to have the fun of editing what I've written. But I do try not to let my professional sticklerism impinge on my daily life—not to natter on at people about the joys of proper grammar and usage. My friends who aren't editors are amused by my obsession with commas and solecisms and dangles and grammatical glitches—I know they see me as the poor doomed herring whose brain has been addled by all that tree-whacking. I recently silenced an entire dinner party when I began to rant about how one of my hapless editing victims doesn't understand the meaning of "Indian summer," which—damn it!—is *not* a warm spell in November but the phenomenon of unseasonably warm weather after a killing frost. If you use it wrongly, you lose the whole bloody concept of Indian summer,[48] which should not be jettisoned along with all the other useful and wonderful English expressions that we've lost because people just don't care enough or pay enough attention to blah blah going to hell in a handbasket yak yak yak the end of civilization as we know it yadda yadda yadda....

When my little diatribe wound down, everyone started talking at once: What's the *problem*, Kitty? Why was that so terrible? Does it really make any difference? That's what they said aloud. I could sense the unspoken—these were, after all, my good friends—subtext:

48 I feel similarly passionate about "the lion's share," which doesn't mean "most of it"—it means "all of it," which is why it's witty. The expression goes back to good old Aesop: the lion goes hunting with the fox, the jackal, and the wolf: they bring down a stag and prepare to divide it. The lion says, "The first quarter is for me because I'm King of Beasts; the second is mine as arbiter; I get the third for my part in the chase; and as for the fourth quarter, I'd like to see which of you will dare to lay a paw upon it."

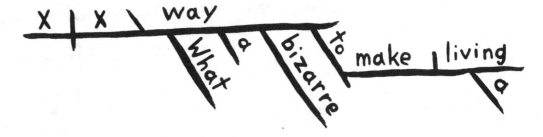

Or something like:

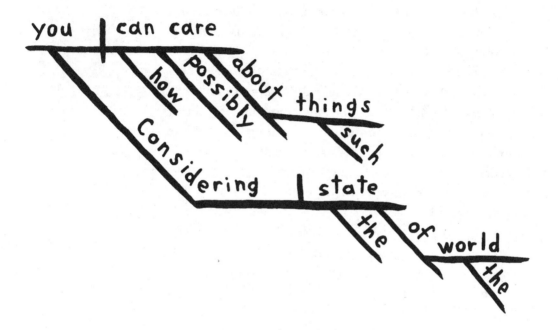

Or, more simply and to the point:

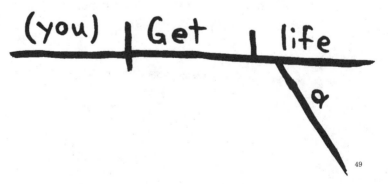

I try, really I do. I no longer say the snooty "It is I," but the cheerily populist "It's me." I've given up on the off-putting "To whom do you wish to speak?" and force myself to say, "Who do ya want?" But it's not easy. I grew up in a richly grammar-infused household. My grandmother forced my scholarly and high-achieving mother, the oldest of eight, to quit high school at sixteen and contribute to the family income—in other words, to trade in her dream of being a Latin teacher for a job on the switchboard in a department store. Her meticulous grammar, her appreciation for a well-turned phrase, her curiosity about words, her apparently inborn gift for perfect spelling, her Latin prizes—even her beautiful handwriting, which persisted unchanged until her extreme old age—were suddenly irrelevant. My mother lived a very long time, but she never got over that disruption in her early life.

But once I was born, she had a pupil-in-residence she could put the teacherly screws to. (She would probably disapprove of that last sentence's final preposition: her formal schooling ended in 1926, when grammarians and teachers were still clinging to the mostly doomed attempt to stuff the unruliness of English into the well-made boxes of Latin and Greek, which is like Cinderella's stepsisters trying to get that glass slipper to fit over their big, ugly bunions.) Mom thought diagramming was the cat's pajamas. I don't know if she learned it in elementary school—she was almost exactly contemporary with Eudora Welty—but it was just the kind of meticulous, practical, and good-for-you activity that she liked, like learning to iron my father's shirts from a pamphlet put out by the government after the war (collar first, front last). I still remember, at age nine, waking up early one morning to find that Mom—who must have checked my homework the night before—had left me a note propped against the Cheerios box. In her firm, disciplined script, it read "I before E except after C." I had never heard this homily before, and I truly thought that my mother had lost her marbles and was now communicating in a code known only to herself and perhaps the crowd of Martians who had taken her over.

I also remember her horror when, at around the same age, I tried to get out the door with "Me and Ann are going over to Barbara's." I was brought back in and given a brief, cogent lesson in Pronouns, Nominative Case of. And another day, when the same Ann got mad at me and accused me of being "too nonchalant," I marched home in a snit and repeated this indignantly to my mother, who had a good laugh—but also took the opportunity to give Ann credit for knowing the word well enough to misuse it.

I have obviously inherited a degree of language snobbery. As a human being, I rejoice in a devil-may-care approach to grammatical correctness. I cherish our dialects, which are one of the few ways left to us of preserving our regional identities.[50] I love ingenious slang terms, wacko clichés (my favorite is "it gets my goat"), and vivid language. Expressions like "that dog don't hunt" and "I could care less" might occasionally pass my own lips (only, of course, when I am under severe stress). But as my mother's daughter and a copy editor to boot, I must officially deplore them all when I find them in print.

50 The South Carolina writer Dorothy Allison commented in an interview: "Do you know what it's like to diagram a Southerner's sentence? You put a Southerner to tell you a story and if you don't rein 'em in at all—it will go on for hours."

I do believe that clarity in speech and precision and consistency in writing will never cease to be important. Language exists so that we can communicate with each other, and surely it continues to be true that—even in a world of email and IM-ing and :) and understaffed classrooms and an anti-elitism that has trickled down from the president himself—we communicate better when we speak and write clearly, and that when we communicate better, we understand each other, and that when we understand each other, life in general is greatly improved.[51] I suppose if I have any rules of writing, they would go something like this:

1. Communicate.
2. Communicate elegantly.
3. When elegance is beside the point, fuhgeddaboutit.

And it's good to remember the importance of context. I speak slightly differently to, say, my landlord than I do to my editor friends, and a smart kid who grew up saying *youse* or *ax* will know not to say "I'm axing youse for a job" at an interview.

As a writer, of course, I try to do my part to keep English accurate and well-scrubbed. Every word I write here is a conscious choice, often deliberated over for much too long.[52] (And I hasten to add that, as Orwell cautioned in "Politics and the English Language": "Look back through this essay and for certain you will find that I have again and again committed the very faults I am protesting against.")

[51] Though there is a certain charm to Gertrude Stein's assertion that "It is not clarity that is desirable but force," which I suppose is a variation on the venerable William Strunk's advice: "If you don't know how to pronounce a word, say it loud."

[52] But, after all, didn't the mighty Flaubert once spend an entire afternoon putting in a comma and the next afternoon taking it out again?

Nobody expects emails to be brilliantly written (though it's fun to get one that is). Everyone has inarticulate moments both in speech and on paper. Every writer, including the great ones, is entitled to the occasional rush of creative momentum that lets slip a grammatical misfortune. And I suppose every copy editor, even Ian McEwan's publisher's copy editor, has moments of sleeping on the job.

But something in me can't deny that these considerations are important, and I don't think I'm a rare bird. Doesn't the world seem to be as full of language snobs as it is of English-abusers? And what if we called them not language snobs or other bad names, but simply reasonable people who want to write clearly and correctly? What else explains the wild popularity of Lynne Truss's best-selling *Eats, Shoots & Leaves?* Or the persistence of William Safire's "On Language" column in *The New York Times* Sunday magazine? Or the emails that deluge bloggers from readers complaining about their use of language? For every careless "me and him went out," or "Express Lane—10 items or less,"[53] or "We except donations" on a sign at the Salvation Army, or "We look forward to hearing your vision, so we can more better do our job,"[54] there's an indignant language nut brandishing an umbrella, and probably writing a book.

But even those of us who appreciate good grammar and proper punctuation and all that don't always respond well to the snotty attitude of some prescriptivists, as exemplified in Truss's ridiculing of what she considers bad English—including the attempts of immigrants to use it

53 Let me put in a vote of thanks for at least two of my local markets, which, bless their hearts, label the express lane "10 items or fewer." I'm hoping this is a trend.

54 George W. Bush, September 20, 2005, Gulfport, Mississippi.

(resulting in such less-than-hilarious errors as "Plum's 49¢ a pound")—an attitude that seems to be deeply beside the point when her own subtitle (*The Zero Tolerance Approach to Punctuation*) is desperately crying out for a hyphen.[55]

I've never been an immigrant, but when I see a lapse in the English used by immigrants, I try to remember my own disastrous forays into other languages. I know a lot of French that disappears when I'm flustered, just enough Italian to get into hot water when I try to speak it, and no Spanish at all (but that doesn't keep me from trying to fake it). I have never really recovered from the Paris waiter who in a voice dripping with *l'horreur* (verging on *la nausée)* informed me (not without Gallic glee) that I had just asked not for a *glass* of wine but a *cup*. Or the waiter in a Perugia café who told me, much more sweetly, that I was referring to my husband as *she*. Or the cleaning woman at a Mexican hotel who patiently endured my interminable and garbled request for an extra blanket, then told me in English that she'd have one on the bed by the time we returned from dinner. So when someone from Pakistan or Romania or China who might not even share our alphabet puts an apostrophe in a funny place, I tend to feel a certain sympathy.[56]

* * *

We've pretty much gotten over the truly silly rules. But there are three common errors that everyone still freaks out over—or over which everyone still freaks out—or maybe over which out of everyone still freaks.

55 I do understand that the British have different punctuational priorities than we do—including not only the hyphen thing but an aversion to the serial comma exemplified in Truss's main title—but that doesn't make them right.

56 In fact, having lived for over a decade in a Polish-Hispanic neighborhood of Brooklyn, I'm never anything less than charmed by signs like "WE DO DUCK WORK" and "ENGLISH SPOKE IN HERE."

57 There's an Australian garage-rock band called The Aints, an offshoot of another Australian garage-rock band called The Saints—which nicely encapsulates the history of the contraction as it traveled over the years from sanctioned to outcast.

1. *Ain't* isn't any more acceptable today than it was for Profs. Reed and Kellogg, who considered it vulgar and said so in no uncertain terms. We're often told—by people who refuse to comprehend that the use of *ain't* marks the beginning of barbarism—that the word wasn't taboo for such venerated 19th-century writers as Jane Austen ("Mind me, now, if they ain't married by Midsummer!") and Anthony Trollope, whose amiably degenerate aristocrats were always complaining, "I'd be happy to pay what I owe you, but I just ain't got the tin." But both those writers used "ain't" only in the speech of characters who were—well, *vulgar*: social-climbing hussies and upper-class twits with drinking problems. For most educated people, *ain't* has long persisted as one of the unforgivable linguistic sins.[57]

58 I found a lovely limerick on the Internet, written by someone identified only as "speedysnail": One word with an undeserved taint / Is surely the infamous ain't. / It's all we have got / To shorten "am not" / As amn't is awfully quaint.

But *ain't* is a sincere attempt to improve the English language. Thanks to some medieval oversight, we don't have a contraction for "am not." There was a flurry of support for "amn't" (young children blurt it out instinctively, and Joyce uses it in *Ulysses*), but for some reason it didn't catch on like "he isn't" and "you aren't."[58] It persisted in England longer than in America (we've always outdone the Brits in terms of primness), and I'm told it's still heard in Ireland and Scotland. But gradually, *ain't,* for legitimate phonological reasons (legitimate but, to me, absolutely opaque, which is why I'm not elaborating) wormed its way into the role and then, at some point in the 19th century, *ain't* too fell out of favor. Now it is universally vilified. Why? Strictly speaking, "he ain't" and "you ain't" are, in fact, incorrect, but "I ain't" is not, if we consider it as a form of "amn't." We have replaced it with the completely illogical "aren't" in constructions like, "I'm right, aren't I?" Anything but *ain't*! Even something twice as wrong! But no one ever said English was rational.[59] As the early grammarians soon found out, Latin it ain't.

As for diagramming an "ain't" construction—well,

$$\underline{\text{It} \mid \text{ain't} \diagdown \text{impossible}}$$

But it's inelegant, confusing, and—worst of all—pointless.

2. Then there is *youse*, which is part of standard speech for several of my aunts, my neighbors, and half the people on the G train out of Brooklyn on a given morning. To me, it's a natural addition to English: it's the plural *you*—our *vous*—and sometimes it seems quite handy.[60] When my aunt Cora asks, "Do youse want a piece of pie?" she's addressing everyone at the table, not just one favored cousin. When my landlord asks me, "So when do youse want me to come up and fix the terlet?"[61] he wants to make it clear that he's fixing the toilet for both my husband and me, not just me—which might sound a bit saucy. In the South, they solve the problem with *y'all*, in a few other parts of America (including West Virginia, Pennsylvania, Texas, and southwestern Ohio), it's *you-uns*,[62] and in the Bible it's *ye*. Waiters faced with a tableful of hungry customers often resort (at least in the kind of restaurants I go to) to something like, "So are you guys ready to order?" It's a little grating—I suspect my *youse*-using aunts would consider "you guys" hopelessly coarse—but it does get around the problem.

59 Don't get me started on "I'm calling from my cell" or "What's your social?"

60 In *The American Language*, H. L. Mencken calls it "a distinction that is well supported by logic and analogy."

61 I would consider my life seriously impoverished if he stopped calling a toilet a *terlet* and that big thing in the cellar *the erl tank*.

62 Check out the song "My Home in San Antone" as sung by Bob Wills & the Texas Playboys, which includes the line: "Where the old folks still say you-uns...."

For all its usefulness, however, *youse* is almost as depraved as *ain't*. H. W. Fowler in *Modern English Usage* (now and for many years one of the sacred texts of language purists) calls *youse* "a low-prestige substitute for the second person plural," and mentions that it's used in such places as Liverpool and Glasgow. He admits that it can be useful for fiction writers, as a kind of short-hand to indicate low class in a character. In *Maggie, a Girl of the Streets*, for example, Stephen Crane has a tough little guy named Jimmie say, "Youse kids make me tired," which diagrams interestingly as:

Youse (kids) |make / tired | me

It's worth noting that by the time Fowler wrote *Modern English Usage* in 1926, when he was 68, he had lived most of his life far from the maelstrom that was actual human speech, in an isolated cottage on the island of Guernsey, relying on the classics for his knowledge of good usage and various newspapers for examples of bad. Despite this seeming handicap, he was a prescriptivist who was surprisingly tolerant and laid back about the language, and he hated snobbery. Fowler, though himself a product of the 19th century (b. 1858), probably would have found Kellogg and Reed and their diagrams a bit stuffy. (Hard to imagine that the man who wrote, "Prefer the familiar word to the far-fetched" and "Prefer the short word to the long" would consider the all too typical Reed-Kellogism "Towers are measured by their shadows, and great men, by their calumniators" an acceptable sentence.) Still, Fowler could be rather out of touch: in his original edition (it has since been revised twice), he deplored what he called a "genteelism," saying *ale* when you mean *beer* because you think *beer* sounds vulgar—unaware, apparently, that they are in fact two distinct beverages.

By comparison, H. L. Mencken, who did for "American" what Fowler did for "English," cited colloquialisms he heard himself on the streets of Baltimore, like " I wisht I had one of them-there Fords" and "I don't work nights no more, only except Sunday nights." (He says, "This last I got from a car conductor.")

Mencken made it clear that he didn't use such substandardisms himself, and I hasten to add that I don't either—at least not often. Even though I admit that there are times when it would make sense to do so, I do not, for example, resort to *youse*. With both my mother and Sister Bernadette hovering in their saintly way somewhere over my head, I find a circumlocution: *Who wants a piece of pie?* In writing, this kind of simple re-wording is often the answer to such gnarly problems. (As Mencken put it, it's only people "of limited linguistic resources" who find them difficult.) But in speech—well, as the great lexicographer (and prose stylist) Samuel Johnson himself said in his 1755 dictionary, "Sounds are too volatile and subtle for legal restraints." But, of course, he didn't know my mother.

Interestingly, there are languages that have a solution to the *youse* ambiguity, or its cousin, the *we* dilemma—languages that go beyond Latin or the Romance languages, or German, or Russian, with their *tu* and *vous* and *voi* and *ty* and *vy* and *du* and *ihr* to indicate singular and plural. None of those languages really tackles the problem. But many Native American languages, including Cherokee and Mohawk, have pronouns that include words for "you and I," "another person and I," "several other people and I," and "you and I plus one other person."

So if my aunt Cora's background was Cherokee instead of Irish, when, in the language of her ancestors, she asked, "Do youse want some hoe cake?"[63] we'd know exactly who was being offered hoe cake and who wasn't.

And, for the record, that question diagrams just as nicely either way:

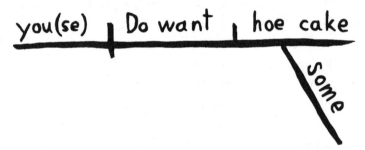

Do you(se) want some hoe cake?

3. *Double negatives.* Unless they're embedded into song titles—"You Ain't Nothin' but a Hound Dog," "I Can't Get No Satisfaction"—or other beloved pop-culture catchphrases ("You ain't seen nothin' yet"), double negatives are right up there with *ain't* and *youse* as markers of seriously low class. (Except for Gertrude Stein, who in her essay on Henry James—well, more or less on Henry James—fearlessly presents us with what may be a

63 "Hoe cake," which was actually baked on a cleaned-off hoe by Indians who had it for lunch as they worked out in the fields—probably usually for a white boss—was a kind of biscuit made with white flour, adapted from a similar cake, using corn, that they made before they were forced onto reservations. As John Winthrop, Jr., the governor of Connecticut, reported back to the members of the English Royal Society in 1662, the Indians actually ate the corn they grew, rather than simply feeding it to their pigs: "Sometimes they bruise it in a mortar and boyle it and make very good food of it, baking it under the embers." The reaction at the Royal Society ranged from incredulity to hilarity.

triple negative: "Not to say this slowly is not to say this not at all." To clarify, she follows up with, "To say this not at all slowly is not not to say this at all.") I remember how clever it seemed when, back in grammar school,[64] we were told that double negatives were unacceptable because they contradicted themselves and ended up saying the opposite of what you mean: they canceled each other out. If you can't get *no* satisfaction, then you must be able to get *some* satisfaction. Right? Sister Bernadette or Miss Peckham would snicker at the absurdity of the very idea. Sister B might even have to get out her trusty ruler and rap the knuckles of the class dunce ("I didn't do nothin'…"). To which (older, wiser, braver) I would respond today: Yes, it makes perfect sense, Sister, except that no one in his right mind would ever misconstrue that sentence, and—*hell*-o?—sentences are not math problems. But—if one does insist on getting mathematical about it—who could deny that a double negative has twice the value of a single one?

And what about the famously language-mad French with their *ne… pas* construction? Presumably it has been approved by the French Academy, an institution that makes Sister Bernadette's uptight linguistic obsessions look like *un pique-nique dans le parc*.

If Mick Jagger had sung "I can't get any satisfaction," he would not have had a hit on his hands. If Elvis had tried to get away with "You are nothing but a beagle," he might very well have gone on working as a truck driver in Memphis instead of being a world-famous rock star who drove around in a custom-made Stutz Blackhawk.[65]

64 Now usually known, less intimidatingly, as elementary or middle school. Originally, grammar schools were so called because there you learned grammar—in those days, Greek and Latin grammar, not your namby-pamby native tongue. In Shakespeare's *Henry VI, Part 2*, the rebel leader Jack Cade lashes out against grammar schools and men who "talk of a noun and a verb, and such abominable words as no Christian ear can endure to hear."

65 During his colorful youth, my husband worked at a car wash in L.A. where he was once privileged to vacuum Elvis's Stutz.

chapter 6

DIAGRAMMING
REDUX

Diagramming has lost much of the cachet it used to claim in education circles when I was in school. Sometime in the '60s, it nearly came to a dead stop. But, like pocket watches and Gilbert & Sullivan operas, the practice persists, alternately trashed and cheered by linguists and grammarians. It's often used in ESL courses, and it's making a small comeback in schools—mostly progressive private ones, but also in public schools here and there around the country. A Cincinnati high-school teacher I talked to insists that "the study of grammar, along with its component of diagramming, helps students become more critical readers and cogent writers." Diagramming can be found lurking in some university linguistics courses, though it's been pretty much superseded by tree diagrams.

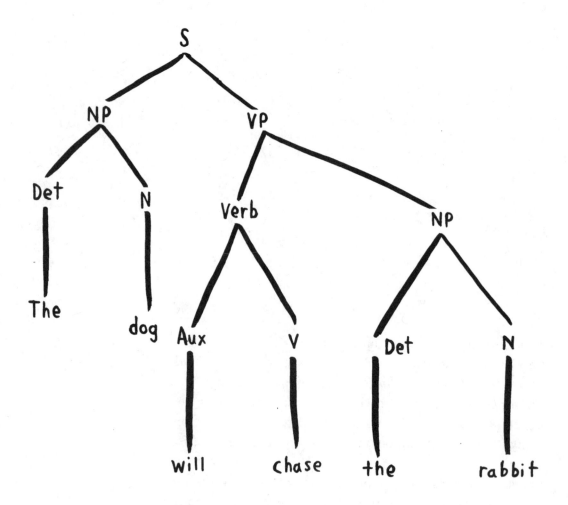

These are considered more complete and, according to a friend of mine who teaches them, easier: traditional diagrams often not only distort the original word order of a sentence, but, as I've mentioned, can also be insanely complex even when they're dealing with a relatively ordinary sentence:

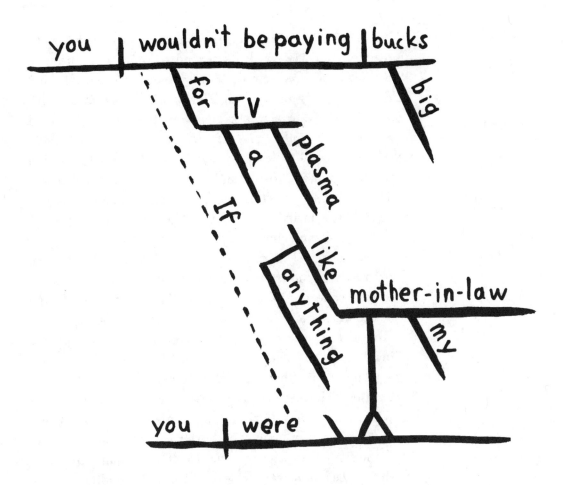

There are diagramming websites run by a few diehard enthusiasts—mostly home-schooling parents—complete with chat rooms and lively disputes about what's the best age for children to begin (the consensus is eleven or twelve). A delightful man named Gene Moutoux (who kindly provided the more difficult diagrams in this book) has a Kellogg-esque moustache, a popular website, and a

Workbook of Sentence Diagramming that's a favorite with teachers and is now in its second edition. In addition to SenDraw, a nifty computer diagramming program from the University of Central Florida that does away with wobbly lines forever, there's a video available called *English Grammar: The Art of Diagramming Sentences* that was made in 1999 but features a very 1950s-looking teacher named Miss Lamb working at a blackboard. The CIA uses some form of diagramming in its computer spyware to clarify and structure the information they get from emails and chat rooms by showing how words relate to each other. (Diagramming will no doubt prevent them from hunting down astronomers or sociologists who email to their colleagues sentences like "The period of revolution of the moons of Jupiter equals the time of their rotation around their axes" or "The sexual revolution exploded into American society like a bomb.")

The most offbeat use of diagramming is in an essay entitled "The Architecture of the Sentence" by the writer William S. Gass (written with his wife, Mary Gass, an architect), in which the authors equate the structure of the sentence with the structure of a building, explaining their thesis in a series of examples that culminate in the "diagramming" of a fiendishly complicated, ingeniously symmetrical sentence by placing it in the rooms of the 1929 McKim, Mead and White floor plan for the Brooklyn Museum.

And perhaps the most practical function of diagramming occurs in a court of law, when, now and then, a grammarian is asked to diagram a sentence in order to elucidate a knotty document, on the assumption that a diagram will make everything clear. However, as Gene Moutoux comments, "One diagrams according to one's understanding of the sentence. Someone understanding a particular sentence differently would necessarily diagram it differently." And he adds, "Meaning does not spring magically from a diagram."

*   *   *

On a slushy Valentine's Day, I stopped in to observe Laura Shearer's seventh graders at a school in Greenwich Village. Every Tuesday, she teaches them grammar—which means she teaches them to diagram sentences. She doesn't know anyone else who does it, but back in Ohio Laura diagrammed sentences herself, loved it, and decided to pass it on.

Why?

"It just makes grammatical ideas clearer," she says. "It's a tool for teaching them how to construct a sentence correctly."

Does it make them better writers?

She dismissed the idea. "Maybe it will make them better editors, but it does *not* improve their writing."

The most important function of diagramming in their lives, though, may be the fun factor. In Laura's opinion, it's good for them in ways that have nothing to do with grammar, or even language. As seventh graders, they're at a transition in their lives as students: they're being asked to become abstract thinkers, and sometimes that's confusing and unsettling—and the onset of puberty, of course, only makes it all worse. "There's so little clarity in their lives at this age," Laura told me, and the wonderful concreteness of diagrams provides some welcome simplicity. "They love this stuff."

The students in Laura's class are enthusiastic, bright, and unintimidated. As they file into the room—chatting, teasing each other, greeting their teacher by her first name—I can't help contrasting them with Sister Bernadette's class, which was silent, cautious, reined in: officially *being good*, which was, more than anything, what parochial schooling in those days was all about. I envy these kids their freedom to be neither bad nor good but just normal.

On the other hand, I have to admit that Sister B had an easier time of it. Laura has to spend the first five minutes just calming them down, and in a 40-minute class, not a lot gets done. ("Have you ever taught?" she asked me. "It's all about patience." Sister B would simply have stood there in her black veil and white wimple and glared at us until we were quiet—except that we were already quiet.) Some of Laura's students are dressed for Valentine's Day, the boys in red t-shirts, the girls in red dresses (one alarmingly low-cut, revealing wishful 12-year-old cleavage) and sporting heart barrettes or jewelry. Again, I think back to my schooldays: the boys wore the usual shirts and trousers to school, but we girls wore maroon serge uniforms that seemed designed to make us look as ungainly as possible, and the school's only concession to Valentine's Day was to let us cut red hearts out of construction paper, print "Have a heart for the missions" on them, and sell them for a nickel apiece to raise money for those worthy missionaries in Africa. Strangers to irony or, apparently, embarrassment, we pinned them to the fronts of our uniforms.

Laura's kids are at a pretty basic stage of diagramming: no long Proustian rambles yet (though Laura assures me they're looking forward to them). The first sentence they deal with is "Does she like pizza and ice cream?" The girl who volunteers to go up to the blackboard makes an artistically perfect diagram

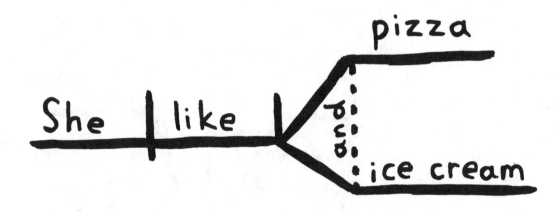

She is gleefully corrected by another student who has noticed she left out the word *does*. Everyone joins in; at this point, Sister B would be getting out her ruler, but Laura remains quietly firm. And eventually they get it right.

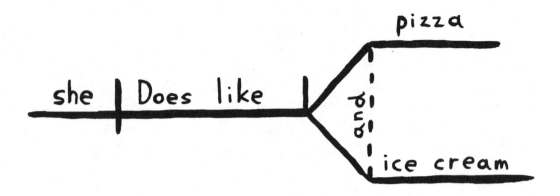

A boy raises his hand. Something has just occurred to him, and he asks excitedly, "How do you diagram *apostrophes*?"

"Not now," Laura tells him—very patiently.

Compounds are the lesson of the day.

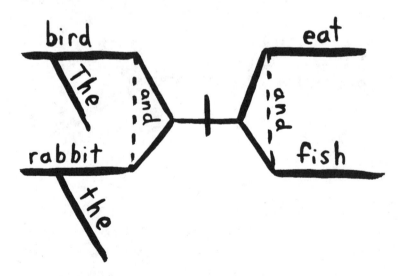

The bird and the rabbit eat and fish.

No one comments on the oddness of a rabbit going fishing. They are concentrating on getting the lines parallel, sometimes resorting to a yardstick and a lot of squinting. They move on to direct objects vs. subject complements—or what, in my day, were called predicate adjectives: *The boy is smart*. The diagrammer makes a mistake, and treats *smart* like a direct object.

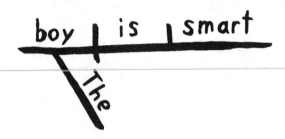

"Direct object?" Laura asks. "Direct object?" Her voice rises. "Remember *I kicked my brother* from last week? Can you kick *smart*?"

"If you kick me, you kick smart," the class smart-alec puts in.

Laura rolls her eyes. Someone slants the offending line properly toward the subject.

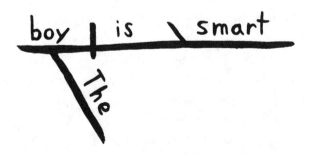

Life goes on. Direct objects are mastered: *Joey ate pie*. "What kind of pie?" someone calls out.

"Cow," says the smart-alec.

When Joey's pie is taken care of, Laura announces that they're going to try something new. Immediately, they are silent, expectant. She draws a blank diagram on the board, and tells them to fill it up. ("You teach them," she tells me later, "and then you let them teach you.") She keeps it simple: she draws a straight line and bisects it with a longer one to separate subject and predicate. Then she draws a shorter perpendicular line, making room for a direct object

A girl wearing a pair of Valentine's Day-red lips pasted to her cheek raises her hand first. "I have a sentence," she says. "But it might be a little offensive."

Laura goes into Sister Bernadette mode. "Offensive? We don't do offensive here."

"Well, it's not *that* offensive," the girl says tantalizingly.

Now everyone wants to know what it is. She goes to the board and fills up the diagram:

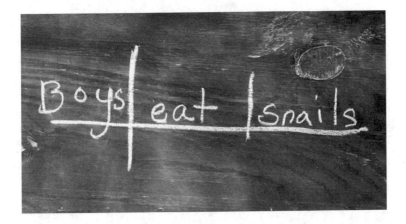

There is a general outcry ("Ew! Gross!") in the midst of which, Laura manages to say, "Good for them! Snails are delicious." More gagging noises, followed by a discussion of snail-eating, and finally, a modification of the sentence by one of the kids:

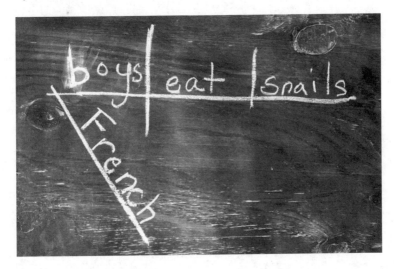

French boys eat snails.

Everyone relaxes.

There is not much time left. The subject of linking verbs is raised. Laura asks, "What's a linking verb?" (I feel a moment of panic: *Don't let her call on me!*) Linking verbs are a problem for a couple of kids; mistakes are made. "I am frustrated," Laura says. "I am mortified. We can't go on to prepositional phrases until every single person in the room gets this." She gives them a homework assignment. "And if you don't remember something, for Pete's sake, go back to your notes. Don't space out on this."

They promise not to space out. She makes them sit quietly for half a minute. They look at her, poised like race-horses at the gate. "Dismissed," she says finally, and they are off.

"They exhaust me," Laura tells me when the room is empty. Then she smiles. "But aren't they great?"

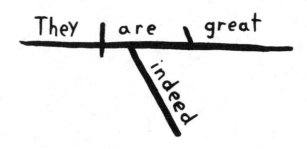

*   *   *

According to the Duchess in *Alice in Wonderland*, "Everything's got a moral if only you can find it." So after all this time immersed in diagramming past and diagramming present, diagramming popular and diagramming vilified, diagramming silly-waste-of-time and diagramming useful-learning-tool, I've managed to find a moral to the story—or at least to draw a few conclusions.

I'm glad sentence diagramming is still, precariously, with us—and not only because I'm at the stage of life where my childhood has taken on a rosy, mythic glow. I think it's probably good for kids, though not for any of the traditional reasons. My memories of Sister B's class are of a form of play that demystified the use of language and all its parts, maybe in the same way that Monopoly taught us about money and greed. Unlike most things we did in school, diagramming had a quality of entertainment.

It also had another virtue. Writing can be terrifying for students in those vulnerable and insecure pre-teen years. This wasn't true for me—I've been shamelessly willing to put my thoughts on paper at the drop of a pencil for as long as I can remember—but for my old sixth-grade friend Rosamond, a blank page was almost as intimidating as the after-school dances the nuns forced us to attend a year or so later, with Buddy Holly blaring tinnily from a portable record player, the boys milling around (staring at their shoes, hands in pockets, snickering) on one side of the room, and the girls (making small-talk, each one wondering miserably why she wore that horrible skirt that makes her look fat and must be the reason no one is dancing with her) on the other.

Rosamond says that, for her, writing was just that ghastly: when "How I Spent My Summer Vacation"-time came around, her hands went clammy and her mind went blank.

But diagramming—that was another world. The only thing that mattered was whether a sentence was diagrammed correctly, and that could be demonstrated to everyone's satisfaction by means of a few intersecting lines. It was a game; it wasn't about *you*. There was no room for opinion. You weren't being judged on the contents of your soul or the quality of your imagination. You weren't writing drivel, you weren't failing to do justice to an idea that gripped you, you weren't afraid of being too fanciful or too dry or too simple-minded—all you needed was accuracy. Brilliant diagramming, unlike brilliant writing, was something that could be learned.

It's debatable whether diagramming did anyone much quantifiable good. For kids with neat handwriting and an artistic sense, it was a chance to show off. For left-brainers who had little interest in English classes, it was a math-like treat. For a shy girl like me, it was an opportunity to perform in public in a small way without knees knocking and sweat rolling down my back. And for a handful of students who simply weren't adept at such things, it was one reinforcement among many of the pesky basics of English. No one learned grammar by diagramming a sentence. It could show us the language at work, with all its nuts and bolts on display, but, if our grasp of grammar hadn't been soundly beaten into us before we ventured on our first wobbly diagrams, Sister B might as well have been teaching her sixth-graders how to paint a sentence in egg tempera or sing it in D-flat major.

Among the people I've talked to about it, the consensus seems to be that learning diagramming may have helped us to understand the functions of words, to think more logically about language, and maybe even to write more correctly. But it didn't help us write well. The admittedly small and eccentric sampling I consulted (half a dozen teachers, a bunch of fiction writers, a screenwriter, a journalist, a couple of editors, two artists, and a gardener) was almost unanimous in believing it did not—though their opinions ranged from "probably didn't hurt" (most) to "irrelevant fun" (many) to "soul-destroying nonsense" (one, who adds, "Patterns and predictability and assigned seating simply don't interest me as much as quirky words and wayward usage."). On home-schooling websites, parents tend to favor diagramming, believing that it helps at least some kids understand what a correct sentence is all about. But the constant refrain is that it all depends on the kid. And teachers who swear by diagramming see it as one useful tool among many.

I'm convinced that diagramming was no help to me at all as a writer. I came out of my 1950s Catholic-school education writing hyper-correct but pretentious, showy, self-conscious prose that had awed my high-school teachers. Great things were predicted for me. Surely this was the work of a Real Writer! Then, in my first year of college, an English professor spent an hour kindly explaining how I could make my writing less stiff and pompous—an hour that I can honestly say changed my life.[66]

There are plenty of valid arguments against diagramming. After all, it doubles the task of the student, who has to learn a whole new set of rules (where does that

66 And the years have shown me that Virginia Woolf's comment on the subject is the real truth: "Style is a very simple matter: all rhythm. Once you get that you can't use the wrong words."

dang-busted line go, and which way does it slant?) in order to illustrate an old set of rules that, in fact, has already been learned pretty thoroughly by immersion in the language from birth. Who's going to make a mistake with a sentence like *The dog barked*? (The barked dog? Dog the barked?) Gertrude Stein makes a good point: English grammar is really quite simple. It's only the subtleties that are difficult—*who* vs. *whom*, adjective vs. adverb, *lie* vs. *lay*. The Internet is full of websites with titles like "The 10 Worst Grammatical Errors in English," and, frankly, they don't amount to much. Surely elaborate diagrams aren't necessary to illustrate them.

It also seems to be true that, over the years, teachers—and certainly students—have become more willing to accept the idea that sentences that can be popped into a diagram aren't always sentences anyone wants to write. And indeed language can be more supple and interesting than the patterns that perfect syntax forces on it. As we've seen, Faulkner and James and Stein and, in fact, most writers at one time or another, have demonstrated the limitations of Sister Bernadette's neatly bundled sentences.

Diagramming isn't dead—it's just resting. The practice is in the process of recovering from the steep slide into marginality that began in the 1960s. Considering the emphasis placed on systemized tasks in education these days, you might think that diagramming—the equivalent of coloring inside the lines—would be clutched to the bosoms of educators with glad little cries. Diagramming prowess, unlike essay-writing, can be measured on standardized tests. But the climb back up is slow. An English teacher I spoke with told me (not happily) that such close attention to the making of correct sentences is now considered dull and dreary—that it interferes with "the full flow of the students' creativity": if they have to think about making every little thing correct, how can they express themselves? As I remember it, the last thing you were expected to do at my school in the '50s was express yourself. You were indeed expected to make every little thing correct, and if you inadvertently expressed yourself in the process—well, Sister Bernadette might just grab you by the ear and drag you to the principal's office.

The '60s are often blamed for the ascendance of "self-expression" and "creativity" over rigor and discipline and the well-wrought sentence, not to mention neatly trimmed hair, premarital chastity, and respect for your elders. During a time when a number of ideas were being weighed in the balance and found wanting (ah, those QUESTION AUTHORITY bumper stickers!), conventional teaching methods didn't escape. Most people would agree that the reading and writing of traditionally correct English have deteriorated since Sister Bernadette's dog began to bark. Maybe we should blame that on the decline of the Reed and Kellogg empire. More likely, we should blame couch potato-ism, a lack of interest in reading literature, the example of our more illiterate public figures, and a general whatever-ism.

But, even if correct English was brought to its knees by those laid-back hippie values, some of the healthier lessons of the '60s have persisted—and a good thing, too.

It was discovered in about 1968 that kids are human and fallible, and most teachers today acknowledge that. They no longer rap knuckles or make students stay after school to do mindless punitive exercises. They probably don't often order them to stand in the wastebasket, as I was made to do in first grade for talking in class ("If you act like trash, Miss Burns, we'll treat you like trash"), or charge them pennies for dropping pencils (fifth grade), or threaten to expel them for saying "heck" (tenth grade). They're a lot more careful now than they were in my schooldays about ridiculing students who are slow to catch on and glorifying the superstars at the expense of everyone else.

The teachers I've talked to who teach diagramming seem to have found a nice balance: the kids are free to express themselves, but they're being taught the skills they need—and diagramming is one aspect of that teaching—to express themselves not only freely but also in correct, intelligible English that's a pleasure rather than a chore to read.

In the end, I think the important thing was not what we learned from diagramming in Sister Bernadette's class, but simply the fun we had doing it. Diagramming made language seem friendly, like a dog who doesn't bark, but, instead, trots over to greet you, wagging its tail.

Sometimes, on a long subway ride or a boring car trip, I mentally diagram a sentence, just as I occasionally try to remember the declension of *hic, haec, hoc* or the words to the second verse of *The Star-Spangled Banner*. And, in an occasional fit of nostalgia and creeping curmudgeonhood, I return to those golden afternoons when

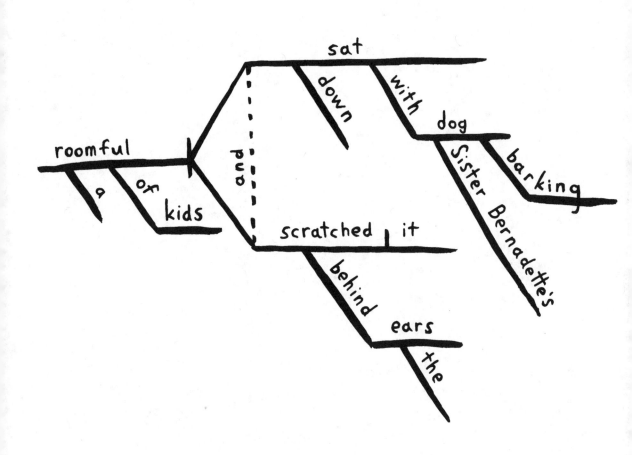

For assistance with the research for this book, my biggest thank-you goes to Gene Moutoux (www.geocities.com/gene_moutoux/), who patiently constructed the difficult diagrams and advised me about the rest. Without Gene, the diagrams here would probably get not only a flunking grade but a rap on the knuckles from Sister Bernadette. Any errors, however, are solely the responsibility of the author.

I am also grateful to Rebecca McFarlan and Laura Shearer.

In addition, thanks to Jessica Auerbach, Rosamond Bennati, Carl Rubino, Ron Savage, the Suffolk County Historical Society, and Heather Walters, the archivist at Polytechnic University (formerly Brooklyn Polytechnic).

This book would not exist without the farsightedness of my publisher, Dennis Johnson, and the intelligence and plain hard work of my editor, Becky Kraemer. I am more grateful to them both than I can express.

KITTY BURNS FLOREY, a veteran copy editor, is the author of nine novels and many short stories and essays. A longtime Brooklyn resident, she now divides her time between central Connecticut and upstate New York with her husband, Ron Savage.